The Coolest Guys

GARY MASON & BARBARA GUNN

Andrews McMeel
Publishing

Kansas City

THE COOLEST GUYS

www.andrewsmcmeel.com

98 99 00 01 02 TRC 10 9 8 7 6 5 4 3 2 1

Library of Congress Cataloging-in-Publication Data on file

Produced by Lionheart Books, Ltd.
Atlanta, Georgia 30341

Design: Jill Dible

Cover photos: Al Bello/Rick Stewart

ATTENTION: SCHOOLS AND BUSINESSES
Andrews McMeel books are available at quantity discounts with bulk purchase for educational, business, or sales promotional use. For information, please write to: Special Sales Department, Andrews McMeel Publishing, 4520 Main Street, Kansas City, Missouri 64111.

Table of Contents

Introduction

It begins, always, on a sheet of ice. It might be the pond in the vacant lot at the end of the block, the one that turns solid as the temperature plummets. It might be the rink at the local community center, the place that dispenses hot chocolate and cranks out the hit parade over the public address system.

It begins, always, with the lacing up of the skates. They might be rentals or they might be your big brother's cast-offs. It doesn't matter.

If you're a little boy with a big dream, they're blades of flying steel. And you aren't some kid on a patch of ice on a deserted lot. You're Gordie Howe, or Rocket Richard or Bryan Trottier.

And this is the National Hockey League.

You might be three or you might be nine when the dream takes root. You might be living in Cranbrook, British Columbia, or in Livonia, Michigan. Or in Bromma, Sweden, or in Moscow.

It doesn't really matter. The dream is still the same. You're not a little boy in a parka and ski pants. You're a finely tuned athlete who can skate at warp speed and stop on a dime. You can dodge anything that comes your way and stick to the puck like a magnet. You're a Montreal Canadien or a Detroit Red Wing or a New York Ranger. You've made it all the way.

And sometimes, sometimes you really do.

Sometimes you fight the staggering odds until you're wearing that jersey for real, not because your mom picked it up at a sportswear sale, but because you earned it fair and square. Because someone saw you and noticed how you really could fly like the wind. Because someone singled you out and decided that you really were good enough to make it to the NHL. But there's a long road between the dream and the achievement. Mike Modano knows that. So do John LeClair and Brendan Shanahan and Alexei Yashin.

Wayne Gretzky knows that you don't become a professional overnight. When you're a kid, you practice hard, sometimes 12 hours a day on the backyard rink. And for some reason, if you really have what it takes, the game will feel more like play than like work.

Steve Yzerman knows, too. He knows that when you're a kid with a passion you sometimes recruit your grandmother as a teammate and pretend the hallway of the house is a hockey rink.

Sometimes, when you're a six-year-old Russian lad named Pavel Bure, you're so determined you put whatever skates are available on your feet, even if they happen to be an old pair of women's figure skates.

Dominik Hasek—he knows about determination, too. He knows you can't relax when your dream is to become the best goaltender in the world. You have to practice, again and again, and you have to study hard. And then you have to practice some more.

But in hockey, practice alone does not make perfect. There's something else that distinguishes the best from the rest. And it has nothing to do with ice time.

Call it drive. Call it determination. Call it that elusive quality that keeps a kid from being a quitter.

It's that trait—whatever you want to call it—that calls on an athlete to win. It's the flash in the eyes of the player who hoists the Stanley Cup.

Joe Sakic has it in abundance. Martin Brodeur has it. And so does Paul Kariya.

Patrick Roy has it in spades—just ask Colorado Avalanche general manager Pierre Lacroix. There are few athletes anywhere, he says, who have the same kind of single-minded thirst for victory that's possessed by the Avalanche goalie.

"That's something you can't invent or create," says Lacroix. "That's something that's inside you, and it's always been inside Patrick."

It's also inside Eric Lindros. The Philadelphia Flyers' captain knows there's only one thing that really matters when you're playing hockey: working your hardest to come out on top.

"Whether's it's the NHL or the Olympics," says Lindros, "the bottom line is winning."

Lindros and his pack of gifted cohorts are not simply superstars. They're the stars of the superstars, the best of the best.

They're the coolest guys on ice.

And even though they've traveled different roads to get where they are, there's no question they've arrived. No matter where their individual journeys began—places like Burnaby, British Columbia, and Riga, Latvia, and Cheshire, Connecticut—today, in many ways, they've reached the same destination.

They are on center stage, standing in the glare of the spotlight. It follows them, game after game, as they blast in the winning goal, or as they knock the puck away from the opponent's net with seconds remaining, or as they make yet another brilliant save to ensure the shutout.

They are standing where the legends stood, guys like Howie Morenz and Guy Lafleur, Gordie Howe and Frank Mahovlich. But today, the screaming from the sidelines isn't for those who've hung up their skates, but for the legends of tomorrow.

It's for today's playmakers, today's record breakers, today's hockey heroes.

It's for the guys who skate their hearts out every night, not because they want to win the Hart Trophy or the Calder or the Vezina, but because that's what superstars do. They play for the team. They play for their fans.

And yes, they play for the fun of it. They're on the ice, not simply because it's their job, but because that's what they've always done. For hours at a stretch.

"We're all big kids at heart, and we all love to play the game," says Wayne Gretzky. "I don't think that ever changes for any player."

Their arenas are no longer frozen ponds. Their skates aren't rentals or hand-me-downs. They're anything but little boys.

And somewhere along the way the most incredible thing happened to their dream. It disappeared, not because it was silly or unrealistic. But because it came true.

Centers of Attention

Spectacular Goals,

Incredible Set-ups,

Winning Key Draws,

and Glass-rattling Hits —

These Guys Are Doing It All

Peter Forsberg

Colorado Avalanche

The story goes like this: Peter Forsberg, a tow-headed Swedish lad of just eight years old, returned home one day in tears.

What's wrong, his father Kent inquired.

"My hockey team lost 8-7 today," Peter said.

"Did you score any of the goals?" asked Peter's dad.

"Yes."

"How many did you score, Peter?"

"Seven."

It's a tale Kent Forsberg is fond of relating. He says it illustrates the way his son has always shunned attention, the way the shy Swede has always thought of the team first and himself second.

But if the 25-year-old Colorado Avalanche center is an uncomfortable superstar, he's a superstar nonetheless.

Many consider Forsberg to be the premier center in the NHL today.

Many consider Forsberg to be the premier center in the NHL today, a remarkable accomplishment for a player named the league's top rookie in 1995. A year later, Forsberg was a Stanley Cup champ, and in 1997 he led Colorado in points with 86 and was named a finalist for the Selke Award, awarded the league's best defensive forward. In 1997–98, he was again the top point man for the Avs, scoring 25 goals and adding 66 assists for 91 points. He was also voted a first-team All-Star center last season.

Consider, too, that he was the first Swedish hockey player to appear on a postage stamp. That honor was bestowed upon Forsberg after he scored the winning goal in the gold-medal shootout round against Canada in the 1994 Lillehammer Olympics.

It's pretty heady stuff, especially considering this is a guy who never even thought about the NHL when he was growing up in Ornskoldsvik, a coastal town of some 60,000, about 375 miles north of Stockholm.

"I didn't even have a goal to play in the [Swedish] elite division," recalls Forsberg, who began skating soon after he learned to walk. "I just tried to work hard and do my best in every practice. That's the way I see hockey—you work hard and then you become better."

Father Kent, who coached Team Sweden—and Peter—in the 1996 World Cup and the 1998 Olympics, remembers how his son was absolutely hooked on hockey from a young age.

"When he was young, it was ice hockey six, seven hours every day. He would go to school, come home only to change clothes so he can go out and skate and play hockey."

And before long the hard work paid off. At 17, Forsberg did make it to the Swedish elite team. In

1991, a month before his eighteenth birthday, he was drafted by the Philadelphia Flyers. He was the Flyers' No. 1 choice, and sixth overall.

A year later, Forsberg became part of the blockbuster trade that saw him moved—along with five other players, two draft picks, and $15 million—to the Quebec Nordiques for the rights to Eric Lindros.

When he arrived in the NHL for the 1994–95 season, Forsberg showed he had considerable skills to offer. He scored 15 goals and made 35 assists in 47 games and won the Calder Memorial Trophy as the league's top rookie. In his second season he accumulated 116 points, fifth highest in the league.

And Forsberg, who relocated to Denver when the Nordiques turned into the Avalanche, soon saw his face appearing on more than just postage stamps.

"He's probably the most complete player in the game," says Avalanche captain Joe Sakic. "He's so strong defensively, and he's so unselfish."

That's quite the compliment, especially when you consider that it comes from another of the top centers in the NHL. It's been said, in fact, that Forsberg and Sakic comprise the NHL's best center pairing since the days when Wayne Gretzky and Mark Messier were Edmonton Oilers.

But if Sakic's game is characterized by his lethal wrist shot, Forsberg's is noted for something else: a grittiness, a toughness, a dazzling ability to stickhandle.

"When Peter has the puck," says Avalanche broadcaster Peter McNab, "you have to cheat to get it from him."

The senior Forsberg says there's also an aggressive element to his son's game. "Peter always played with older guys, and he wanted to show them he could give a hit and take a hit," says Kent Forsberg. "Sometimes he was a little too physical."

Ask former Avalanche coach Marc Crawford what makes Forsberg go, and he'll tell you it comes down to basic determination.

"He wants to be the best," says Crawford. "He wants his team to be the best, and he's going to do whatever it takes to make sure he's successful."

And that's the simple truth. Peter Forsberg is no longer the the eight-year-old who came home in tears after a hockey game one day. But one thing is as strong as it was back then: the hunger for victory.

"I can't stand losing," he says.

#21 PETER FORSBERG, Colorado Avalanche, center

YEAR	TEAM	LEA	REGULAR SEASON					PLAYOFFS				
			GP	G	A	TP	PIM	GP	G	A	TP	PIM
1990-91	MoDo	Swe.	23	7	10	17	22	.....	.....	.....	.....	.....
1991-92	MoDo	Swe.	39	9	18	27	78	.....	.....	.....	.....	.....
1992-93	MoDo	Swe.	39	23	24	47	92	3	4	1	5	0
1993-94	MoDo	Swe.	39	18	26	44	82	11	9	7	16	14
1994-95	MoDo	Swe.	11	5	9	14	20	.....	.....	.....	.....	.....
	Quebec	NHL	47	15	35	50	16	6	2	4	6	4
1995-96	Colorado	NHL	82	30	86	116	47	22	10	11	21	18
1996-97	Colorado	NHL	65	28	58	86	73	14	5	12	17	10
1997-98	Colorado	NHL	72	25	66	91	94	7	6	5	11	12

Jeff
Friesen

San Jose Sharks

It's a thrill for any player to score a goal in the National Hockey League.

But to score that goal shorthanded and watch it become the game-winner, is something else indeed. Especially when it's your first-ever goal in the NHL and when the game is televised and the whole family is watching.

It was back in 1995, and the player was San Jose's Jeff Friesen, at 18, the youngest player in the league that year.

Friesen, who'd been picked eleventh overall by the Sharks in the entry draft the previous June, landed instantly in the hockey spotlight with his goal in that match against Toronto. And he remained the center of attention for the rest of the year, finishing fourth in the rookie of the year balloting by scoring 25 points in 48 games.

> ## "This year, Jeff has declared himself."
> —Tony Granato

"My rookie year was a good year for me," says Friesen. "I was surrounded by a lot of people who supported me and gave me confidence. I knew, though, that I was a long way from reaching my utmost potential."

Today, at just 22, the speedy left winger from Meadow Lake, Saskatchewan, is regarded as the Sharks' fastest skater and most talented offensive player. In 1997–98, the season in which he suffered a separated shoulder, he led his team in points, with 63, and scored 31 goals to tie the franchise mark set by Owen Nolan.

But then, scoring goals has always been what The Freeze is about.

In one year with the Regina Pats of the Western Hockey League, he netted 51 goals and added 67 assists to finish with 118 points. The previous year he had 45 goals and 38 assists, to end up with 83 points.

No wonder the Sharks sat up, took notice, and recruited the sharpshooter.

Friesen has had many other great hockey memories: he played for the gold medal–winning Team Canada at the 1997 World Championships in Finland, for the silver medal–winning Canadian team a year earlier in Vienna, Austria, and in 1995 helped the Canadian World Junior team defeat the heavily favored Russians to take the gold medal.

But Friesen says the day he was drafted into the NHL ranks up there among the best days of his life. He signed on the dotted line, then paid off some of his parents' bills and went shopping for a couple of satellite dishes so his parents and grandparents could keep tabs on all his games.

Today, observers agree, Friesen has responded to the tough demands of coach Darryl Sutter and developed into a reliable team player.

"There is a pivotal time in every player's career when he either levels off, drops down, or takes that next step everyone talks about," says Sharks left wing Tony Granato. "This year, Jeff has declared himself."

Friesen says Sutter has challenged him every step of the way—and he wouldn't want it any other way.

"When I do something wrong, he certainly isn't shy about telling me. But I'd think anybody would want to know where they stand with a coach, rather than spend all your time guessing. He's challenged me to see what kind of player I am."

That kind of player is one who's gritty, quick, and smart on the ice.

"This is one of the premier hockey players," says *Hockey Night in Canada* commentator Don Cherry. "He's the fastest skater—I don't care what anybody says—when he has the puck."

Bernie Nicholls, a veteran center with the Sharks, couldn't agree more.

"The best thing about Jeff's game is he wants to do well, he wants to be a successful player," says Nicholls. "You can go through life and be an average player, or you can be great. Jeff wants to be the best player on the team."

As coach Sutter sees it, Friesen probably is.

"I know the talent level he has—he's probably our most skilled player," says Sutter. "The big thing with Jeff is he's tried to make a commitment to be an all-

round player. Better defense—more concentration."

Friesen readily admits the coach is right. He can recall a day, in junior hockey, when he felt his only job was to score goals. But now he recognizes that he can both score and be a defensive threat at the same time. Ultimately, he says, it all comes down to the drive to win.

"My focus now is on playing the best hockey of my career," says Friesen. "I want to play a role in helping the team win—that's where I'm at now. I want to win games."

#39 JEFF FRIESEN, San Jose Sharks, center

			REGULAR SEASON					PLAYOFFS				
YEAR	TEAM	LEA	GP	G	A	TP	PIM	GP	G	A	TP	PIM
1991-92	Regina	WHL	4	3	1	4	2	.....	.....	.....	.....	.....
1992-93	Regina	WHL	70	45	38	83	23	13	7	10	17	8
1993-94	Regina	WHL	66	51	67	118	48	4	3	2	5	2
1994-95	Regina	WHL	25	21	23	44	22	.....	.....	.....	.....	.....
	San Jose	NHL	48	15	10	25	14	11	4	5	6	4
1995-96	San Jose	NHL	79	15	31	46	42	.....	.....	.....	.....	.....
1996-97	San Jose	NHL	82	28	34	62	75	.....	.....	.....	.....	.....
1997-98	San Jose	NHL	79	31	32	63	40	6	0	1	1	2

Wayne Gretzky

New York Rangers

The news was news to no one. In early 1998, when the *Hockey News* pronounced Wayne Gretzky the greatest hockey player of all time, it was like announcing that ice is cold. We knew it already.

The respected hockey bible had surveyed some 50 hockey experts to arrive at its decision, and in the end, Gretzky edged out both Bobby Orr and Gordie Howe to be named best player ever to hold a hockey stick.

The Great One became The Greatest One.

In style typical of the classy 37-year-old, Gretzky was humbled by the poll.

"To be No. 1 is very special," said the New York Rangers center. "To be honest, I'm embarrassed. If I had been voted behind Bobby Orr or Gordie Howe, I would've been happy to be third. I say that with all

sincerity because they're the guys I looked up to when I was growing up."

When Gretzky was growing up, folks had only to get a glimpse of the kid to know he possessed a kind of unworldly hockey ability. When he was six, after all, he was playing against 10-year-olds. And when he reached 11, don't forget, he scored 378 goals in 69 games. Gretzky wasn't talented, he was supernatural.

It was in Brantford, Ontario, that Gretzky first put his blades to ice—at the tender age of two. Father Walter, who never missed one of his son's practices, or any of his games, built the best back-yard rink in the area. "Wally's Coliseum," as it was known, was 20 feet wide and 35 feet long, and the ice was seven inches thick.

When there were no records left to break, he broke and rebroke his own records.

On weekends, Gretzky would be out there from 7 a.m. until 7:30 p.m., coming in only to watch *Hockey Night in Canada*. It was the place where Wayne grew up.

Sports, recalls Wayne, was the thing his father valued more than anything—except, of course, for family.

"We never went on holidays because he wanted all the money to be put toward athletics and that kind of stuff. When I was eight years old, I remember my mom, Phyllis, saying, 'I need a new set of curtains.' And my dad said, 'Hang a couple of sheets up. We gotta get Wayne a new pair of skates.' "

It was immediately after Gretzky's unbelievable 378-goal season—he won the scoring race by 238 goals that year—the hockey world sat up and took notice. As one journalist observed, "He went from Brantford boy to world prodigy in the space of a year."

Gretzky became sought-out in the media circuit. One newspaper writer from London, Ontario, John Herbert, dubbed him The Great Gretzky, a name that soon evolved into The Great One.

At the age of 17, Gretzky signed his first pro contract with the WHA. He played just eight games of the 1978-79 season with the Indianapolis Racers, and was then sold to the Edmonton Oilers, at that time part of the WHA.

At 18, he was handed rookie of the year honors for his 43 goals and 61 assists. And that was just the beginning.

In Gretzky's first four years with the Oilers—which by then had joined the NHL—No. 99 posted point totals of 137, 164, 212, and 196. He stayed above the 200-point mark over the next three years, hitting 205, 208, and then an unbelievable 215. That marker was better than any previous player's by a staggering 63 points.

"People like to say he's the Michael Jordan of our sport, but I disagree," says Glen Sather, Gretzky's first coach in Edmonton.

"Before Jordan there was Larry Bird and Magic Johnson and Dr. J. Well, I look at Wayne as being a bit of all those guys rolled into one. He's our sport's greatest superstar, and he has singlehandedly lifted this league to where it is now."

There is simply no arguing that. It was during Gretzky's seven-plus years with the L.A. Kings, for instance, that average attendance was some 4,400 above the levels in the pre-Gretzky era. In fact, the biggest crowd ever to see an NHL game was one that involved Gretzky. A total of 25,581 people turned out one night in September, 1990, to watch Gretzky's Kings play an exhibition game in a domed baseball stadium in St. Petersburg, Florida.

Today, Gretzky, who's played with the St. Louis Blues in addition to the Oilers, the Kings, and the Rangers, is a hockey player with four Stanley Cups to his credit, and who has shattered 61 NHL records. He's won the league's Most Valuable Player award nine times.

"When there were no records left to break, he broke and rebroke his own records," notes one observer. So astonishing is Gretzky that even if he had never scored a goal during his career, he'd still be the NHL's top leader in points.

Even today, as Gretzky nears the conclusion of his hockey career, he's still leading the pack. In 1997–98 he led the Rangers with 23 goals and 67 assists for 90 points.

He is, without question, the irrefutable master of hockey, a man who has revolutionized the game with his awesome playmaking abilities and his

uncanny manner of dancing through every player on the ice.

"Wayne is from a different planet than all of us," says Sather. "How do you describe genius?"

#99 WAYNE GRETZKY, New York Rangers, center

YEAR	TEAM	LEA	REGULAR SEASON					PLAYOFFS				
			GP	G	A	TP	PIM	GP	G	A	TP	PIM
1978-79	Indianapolis	WHA	8	3	3	6	0	.....	.....	.....	.....	.....
	Edmonton	WHA	72	43	61	104	19	13	10	10	20	2
1979-80	Edmonton	NHL	79	51	86	137	21	3	2	1	3	0
1980-81	Edmonton	NHL	80	55	109	164	28	9	7	14	21	4
1981-82	Edmonton	NHL	80	92	120	212	26	5	5	7	12	8
1982-83	Edmonton	NHL	80	71	125	196	59	16	12	26	38	4
1983-84	Edmonton	NHL	74	87	118	205	39	19	13	22	35	12
1984-85	Edmonton	NHL	80	73	135	208	52	18	17	30	47	4
1985-86	Edmonton	NHL	80	52	163	215	46	10	8	11	19	2
1986-87	Edmonton	NHL	79	62	121	183	28	21	5	29	34	6
1987-88	Edmonton	NHL	64	40	109	149	24	19	12	31	43	16
1988-89	Los Angeles	NHL	78	54	114	168	26	11	5	17	22	0
1989-90	Los Angeles	NHL	73	40	102	142	42	7	3	7	10	0
1990-91	Los Angeles	NHL	78	41	122	163	16	12	4	11	15	2
1991-92	Los Angeles	NHL	74	31	90	121	34	6	2	5	7	2
1992-93	Los Angeles	NHL	45	16	49	65	6	24	15	25	40	4
1993-94	Los Angeles	NHL	81	38	92	130	20	.....	.....	.....	.....	.....
1994-95	Los Angeles	NHL	48	11	37	48	6	.....	.....	.....	.....	.....
1995-96	Los Angeles	NHL	62	15	66	81	32	.....	.....	.....	.....	.....
	St. Louis	NHL	18	8	13	21	2	13	2	14	16	0
1996-97	NY Rangers	NHL	82	25	72	97	28	15	10	10	20	2
1997-98	NY Rangers	NHL	82	23	67	90	28	.....	.....	.....	.....	.....

Eric Lindros

He's been called The Presence. He's been called An Event. He's been called big, tough, and forceful, a hockey leader who ranks as one of the best players in the world today.

Off the ice, he's been described as gentle and soft-spoken, a guy who's active in charitable events, who's a pushover with the kids.

Eric Lindros is something else.

"He's the total package," says Philadelphia left winger John LeClair, once part of the vaunted Legion of Doom, a trio that included Lindros and right winger Mikael Renberg.

Clearly, Lindros is a hockey player who can't be

> "When he hits you he can hurt you. No, check that . . . he can kill you."
> —Theo Fleury

ignored. His size, if anything, ensures that. The 25-year-old native of London, Ontario, stands 6' 4" and weighs 236 pounds.

He's huge—in more ways than one.

"He is a big, strong hockey player who can lead the league in points and be a physical dimension in every game every night," says Calgary Flames coach Brian Sutter. "What more is there?" Not much.

At the end of the 1997–98 regular season, the Philly captain ranked right up there among the top point men on the Flyers. He scored 30 goals and added 41 assists for 71 points. The previous season—the year the Flyers made it all the way to the Stanley Cup Finals—Lindros accumulated 79 points, in spite of missing 30 games due to injuries. A year earlier, his total was 115.

How good is No. 88? Good enough that he's one of the top wage-earners in the league.

Good enough that in his final year of junior hockey in Ontario, he posted 71 goals and 78 assists and earned the nickname The Next One—the heir apparent to Wayne Gretzky.

Good enough—and popular enough—that he was recruited to appear on *Late Night with David Letterman*. He is, observes sports writer George Johnson, hockey's biggest attraction.

"Lindros isn't a subtly shaded art house film, he's a $200-million special effects epic," says Johnson. "He isn't an intensely personal novella. He's a sprawling, best-selling page-turner."

Calgary's Theo Fleury, who first played alongside Lindros at the 1991 Canada Cup, says Lindros has something you don't see often in a hockey player: "His size and his strength. He is so much stronger than every one else it's a joke," says Fleury. "When he hits you he can hurt you. No, check that . . . he can kill you."

Eric Lindros is something else, indeed. Yet there was a time, not so long ago, when a career as a professional athlete wasn't something he counted on.

"I didn't know I was going to be a pro player," recalls Lindros. "When I was 16 or 17 I thought I had a shot at this and I got lucky."

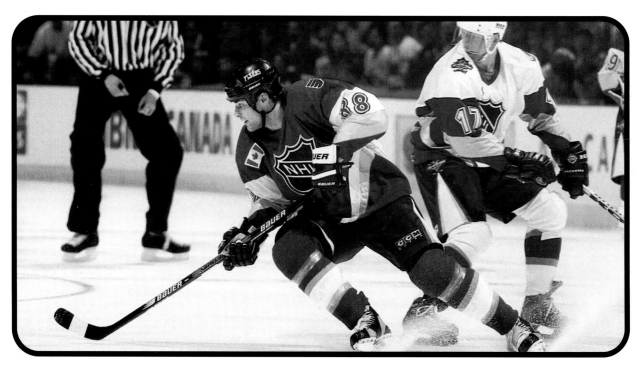

Some, however, will argue that luck had little to do with Lindros's entry into the NHL. Raw talent, certainly. Luck, probably not.

In 1991, after playing junior for several years, Lindros was drafted by the Quebec Nordiques, their No. 1 choice, and first overall. He returned to junior hockey and a year later went to Philadelphia as part of one of the biggest trades in NHL history. He was exchanged for Mike Ricci, Steve Duchesne, Ron Hextall, Peter Forsberg, Chris Simon, Kerry Huffman, two future first-round draft picks, and $15 million.

In 1994–95, Lindros won the Hart Trophy as the league's MVP. He's won the Lester B. Pearson Award and the Bobby Clarke Trophy. He's played on NHL All-Star teams and for Team Canada in its ride to the 1991 Canada Cup championship, something Lindros puts down as his greatest hockey memory.

But there are other hockey memories among Lindros's stash that don't cast the shine he'd hoped they would. The burly center, whose single-minded determination to win has been equated to that of Tiger Woods, traveled to Nagano, Japan, in early 1998 as captain of Team Canada, determined to return with a piece of gold. The team returned with no medal at all.

It was the second time in less than a year that victory had eluded Lindros. It was Detroit, not

Philadelphia, that ended up taking the Stanley Cup in 1997, its first win since 1955.

Still, there are other cups to be won, and Lindros is determined to take one for Philly.

"The focus is on winning a cup for this city and the fans who were supportive of us since I got here, through the lean years," he says. "People stuck behind us. I know everybody in that dressing room wants a cup for this city."

And winning, says Lindros, is all that really matters.

#88 ERIC LINDROS, Philadelphia Flyers, center

YEAR	TEAM	LEA	REGULAR SEASON					PLAYOFFS				
			GP	G	A	TP	PIM	GP	G	A	TP	PIM
1988-89	Cdn. National Jr.	.....	2	1	0	1	0	.....	.....	.....	.....	.....
1989-90	Det. Comp.	USHL	14	23	29	52	123	.....	.....	.....	.....	.....
	Cdn. National Jr.	.....	7	4	0	4	4	.....	.....	.....	.....	.....
	Oshawa	OHL	25	17	19	36	61	17	18	18	36	76
1990-91	Oshawa	OHL	57	71	78	149	189	16	18	20	38	93
	Cdn. National Jr.	.....	7	6	11	17	6	.....	.....	.....	.....	.....
1991-92	Oshawa	OHL	13	9	22	31	54	.....	.....	.....	.....	.....
	Cdn. National Jr.	.....	24	19	16	35	34	.....	.....	.....	.....	.....
	Cdn.Olympic	.....	8	5	6	11	6	.....	.....	.....	.....	.....
1992-93	Philadelphia	NHL	61	41	34	75	147	.....	.....	.....	.....	.....
1993-94	Philadelphia	NHL	65	44	53	97	103	.....	.....	.....	.....	.....
1994-95	Philadelphia	NHL	46	29	41	70	60	12	4	11	15	18
1995-96	Philadelphia	NHL	73	47	68	115	163	12	6	6	12	43
1996-97	Philadelphia	NHL	52	32	47	79	136	19	12	14	26	40
1997-98	Philadelphia	NHL	63	30	41	71	134	5	1	2	3	17

Mike Modano

Dallas Stars

When Mike Modano was a youngster in Michigan, people had only to look at him on the ice to recognize that there was something different about the kid.

They had only to hear his mom talk about how he convinced her to join him in puck practice in the basement of the family home, and how she'd use garbage lids to protect herself.

Here was a kid who left home at the age of 16 to play hockey in Prince Albert, Saskatchewan, a hockey player who accumulated 127 points in one of his three seasons there, and 105 in another. Anyone who'd paid any attention when the boy from Livonia was growing up would have known: the kid had talent.

He did, and he does.

At 28, he's the star of the Dallas Stars, a guy whose reputation is built around speed, agility, and an uncanny ability to control a hockey puck.

"He's probably the best in the league as far as pure passing," says Modano's teammate, left wing Greg Adams. "I mean [Wayne] Gretzky is probably more creative, but just the skill of passing, no one's better than Mo.

> "He's probably the best in the league as far as pure passing," says Modano's teammate, left wing Greg Adams.

"There are guys who might be able to skate as fast as him, but to control the puck and do the things he does at top speed, very few can do that."

Modano, who went first overall in the NHL's 1988 Entry Draft, had his best-ever year with the Stars in 1993–94, when he hit the 50-goal mark and helped Dallas to its best finish in franchise history. But if that was his best season, the following would be among his most disappointing. Modano injured his left ankle in

a match against Vancouver, and ended up missing 14 regular season games and the playoffs.

"This injury was the worst I've ever had in my career," recalls Modano. He underwent surgery to repair two ruptured tendons, and was then forced to watch from the sidelines as Dallas was dropped from the playoffs.

But the rehab was in full swing that summer: Modano concentrated hard on his recovery, determined to lead his team again, and not to be defeated by his injury.

"No one wants to sit out for a long period of time," he says. "It's frustrating to have to sit there and watch, it drives you to work harder."

The work paid off. The following season Modano led the Stars with 36 goals and 45 assists for 81 points. The next year he did even better, lifting his point total to 83.

These days, when Modano thinks back to how his game has evolved, he acknowledges that it's changed considerably.

"I was frustrated a lot in the past," he says. "[General Manager] Bob Gainey brought me along slowly. He wanted me to watch and learn, and I sure did a lot of watching and learning."

Dallas coach Ken Hitchcock says Modano has developed enormously, a direct result of the center's commitment and determination. Modano is still a scoring machine, but he's come to realize that hockey is about teamwork more than anything else.

"You can tell he's a determined player," says Hitchcock. "But I think his determination comes from wanting to play well and wanting the team to play well, not from trying to score."

If Modano has become cherished by his teammates—for five years, the team has voted him winner of the Bill Masterton Award as MVP—he's also become cherished by his community. In 1994–95 he earned the Stars Community Service Award in recognition of his tireless devotion to fundraising, primarily for cerebral palsy.

He's also developed a presence outside the hockey circle. Most players in the NHL are accustomed to seeing their mugs inside the pages of such publications as *Hockey News*, but Modano's face has appeared elsewhere: in *Cosmopolitan*, in *Mademoiselle*, in *Marie Claire*. Not long ago, he was also voted one of the 10 sexiest people in Dallas by *D Magazine*.

Atoosa Behneghr, Senior Fashion Editor of *Cosmopolitan* magazine, sees more than a hockey player when she sees Mike Modano.

"In terms of mainstream appeal, Mike Modano has it all: presonality, good looks, and superior ath-letic ability. Obviously, he's become a particular draw for women hockey fans across the country."

Clearly, the spotlight has come to shine brightly on Mike Modano, now also a veteran of Olympic competition, having traveled to Nagano with the U.S. hockey team in 1998. He has come a long way since he started out in Michigan, but one thing hasn't changed at all: his talent on the ice.

#9 MIKE MODANO, Dallas Stars, center

| YEAR | TEAM | LEA | REGULAR SEASON | | | | | PLAYOFFS | | | | |
			GP	G	A	TP	PIM	GP	G	A	TP	PIM
1986-87	Prince Albert	WHL	70	32	30	62	96	8	1	4	5	4
1987-88	Prince Albert	WHL	65	47	80	127	80	9	7	11	18	18
1988-89	Prince Albert	WHL	41	39	66	105	74	.....	.....	.....	.....	.....
	Minnesota	NHL	.....	.....	.....	.....	.....	2	0	0	0	0
1989-90	Minnesota	NHL	80	29	46	75	63	7	1	1	2	12
1990-91	Minnesota	NHL	79	28	36	64	65	23	8	12	20	16
1991-92	Minnesota	NHL	76	33	44	77	46	7	3	2	5	4
1992-93	Minnesota	NHL	82	33	60	93	83	.....	.....	.....	.....	.....
1993-94	Dallas	NHL	76	50	43	93	54	9	7	3	10	16
1994-95	Dallas	NHL	30	12	17	29	8	.....	.....	.....	.....	.....
1995-96	Dallas	NHL	78	36	45	81	63	.....	.....	.....	.....	.....
1996-97	Dallas	NHL	80	35	48	83	42	7	4	1	5	0
1997-98	Dallas	NHL	52	21	38	59	32	17	4	10	14	12

Keith Primeau

Carolina Hurricanes

Carolina Hurricanes center Keith Primeau demonstrated early in life he was one tough hockey player.

It was during a minor hockey tournament in Ottawa that young Keith raised his arms in celebration after scoring a goal. At that very moment, a tough guy from the Boston team playing against Primeau knocked him to the ice. Keith's collarbone was cracked.

After only a month, Keith's team was due to play in a tournament in Boston. There was no way he was going to miss it. "You bet he made it back for it," recalls Primeau's dad, Mike. "He was looking

"He can skate, he can hit, he's very intense, and he's a large man—which makes him a key defensive center."
—Paul Maurice

for that guy who cracked his collarbone and he just flattened him at center ice. I thought, 'Well, I guess his collarbone is all right.'"

Keith Primeau, all 6' 5" inches, 220 pounds of him, has been leaving people flat on the ice ever since. Now in his seventh full NHL season, Primeau is rounding into one of the best power forwards in the game.

"Keith's best qualities are not necessarily scoring goals," says Hurricanes coach Paul Maurice. "He can skate, he can hit, he's very intense, and he's a large man—which makes him a key defensive center."

Primeau, 26, takes his role as Carolina captain seriously. No one works harder before or after games in an effort to get an edge. A couple of hours

before game time, you'll often find Primeau running up and down the steps in the Greensboro Coliseum where the Hurricanes currently play their games.

"We lose a game, Keith is in the room the next day, and he's riding the bike, he's on the treadmill, he's working out, he skates by himself after—it's almost like he's whipping himself for the loss," says Maurice.

"Sometimes, I'm not so sure that's the best thing for him because he plays so many minutes."

This past season, Primeau led his team with 26 goals and 37 assists for 63 points. He also piled up 110 penalty minutes. He was also instrumental in leading his team in a surprising late-season charge for a playoff spot—a charge that fell just short.

Primeau played his junior hockey in Niagara Falls, Ontario. On the last day of his junior season, Primeau was so sick with the flu he could barely lace up his skates. He was also in a dogfight with Mike Ricci for the Ontario Hockey League scoring title. He turned to his mother, Peg, for advice. "You might not have another chance in your life to win something like this," she told him. "So try your best and have no regrets." He had five points in that game to clinch the title. He would have no regrets.

"Peg and I always used to say to all the kids: 'If you get involved with something, you see it through,'" says Mike Primeau, an Ontario Hydro supervisor. "'If there is any adversity, fight your way through it. When it's over, and you don't want to go back to it, fine. But if you start something, you finish it.'"

"I was never pushed to do anything," Keith remembers of his youth. "I was allowed to try anything I wanted—but I didn't take to everything. Hockey seemed to be the one thing I did take to."

Primeau would be a much-heralded first-round draft pick (third overall) of the Detroit Red Wings in the 1990 Entry Draft. He was viewed as the type of player the Wings needed to end their Stanley Cup drought. But the relationship would end unhappily. The Detroit organization and many of its fans believed Primeau wasn't scoring enough and wasn't hitting enough either. For his part, Primeau was tired of playing on the third line. He asked to be traded, and on October 9, 1996, he got his wish, landing in Hartford, which would later relocate to North Carolina.

"I have no regrets," says Primeau of the move. "I just made what I felt was the right move for my hockey career. I wanted to go to a team where I was going to get a chance to play and a chance to be a leader."

Primeau admits it was tough watching the Wings win the Stanley Cup in 1996–97, but his pain was softened somewhat when he joined Team Canada at the World Championships the same year and won gold.

Primeau's younger brother, Wayne, plays in the NHL for the Buffalo Sabres. The two were dubbed the "Battling Primeaus" when they found themselves paired off and exchanging punches in one game a couple of seasons back.

Keith was upset and immediately went to the Carolina dressing room and phoned home. "I called my dad and he was laughing," Keith remembers. "In the background I could hear my mom and my mom was mad, so my dad's tone changed rather rapidly."

Primeau was selected to play on Canada's Olympic team in Nagano. While Canada failed to meet the high expectations that had been established, Primeau was one of his country's best players. And along the

way he impressed one of the best in the game.

"Obviously when you score goals it brings a lot of attention," says Philadelphia Flyers captain Eric Lindros. "But to win key faceoffs, make big checks, there's a lot of other variables that make a great hockey player. When you look at Keith Primeau, you're looking at a great hockey player."

#55	**KEITH PRIMEAU**, Carolina Hurricanes, center											
			REGULAR SEASON					**PLAYOFFS**				
YEAR	TEAM	LEA	GP	G	A	TP	PIM	GP	G	A	TP	PIM
1987-88	Hamilton	OHL	47	6	6	12	69	.....	.....	.....	.....	.....
1988-89	Niagara Falls	OHL	48	20	35	55	56	17	9	16	25	12
1989-90	Niagara Falls	OHL	65	57	70	127	97	16	16	17	33	49
1990-91	Detroit	NHL	58	3	12	15	106	5	1	1	2	25
	Adirondack	AHL	6	3	5	8	8	.....	.....	.....	.....	.....
1991-92	Detroit	NHL	35	6	10	16	83	11	0	0	0	14
	Adirondack	AHL	42	21	24	45	89	9	1	7	8	27
1992-93	Detroit	NHL	73	15	17	32	152	7	0	2	2	26
1993-94	Detroit	NHL	78	31	42	73	173	7	0	2	2	6
1994-95	Detroit	NHL	45	15	27	42	99	17	4	5	9	45
1995-96	Detroit	NHL	74	27	25	52	168	17	1	4	5	28
1996-97	Hartford	NHL	75	26	25	51	161	.....	.....	.....	.....	.....
1997-98	Carolina	NHL	81	26	37	63	110	.....	.....	.....	.....	.....

Joe Sakic

Colorado Avalanche

He is, some say, an anomaly among professional athletes. He doesn't seek out the spotlight. At times, he tends even to avoid it.

Joe Sakic is pretty much your Ordinary Joe.

Except, of course, that there's nothing remotely ordinary about the 29-year-old captain of the Colorado Avalanche. He's a Stanley Cup champion, a Conn Smythe Trophy winner, and now, an Olympian.

He's also one of the most unassuming, most down-to-earth guys around.

"What you get with Joe is what he is," says former teammate Uwe Krupp. "He is extremely humble. It's just the way he is. He thinks only of the team. He's about the most unselfish person I know. He's not into that self-congratulatory stuff you see with a lot of stars in a lot of sports."

> ## "What you get with Joe is what he is," says former teammate Uwe Krupp. "He is extremely humble."

Humble, yes. Thoughtful, certainly.

And as a hockey player, unbelievably talented.

Joe Sakic has been hooked on the ice rink since that day in the mid-70s when mother Marijan took him to his first NHL game. They lived in Burnaby, British Columbia, a bedroom community east of

Vancouver, and they had tickets to a showdown at the Pacific Coliseum between the Canucks and the Atlanta Flames. Sakic was just five years old.

Their seats, recalls Sakic, were "way up in the nosebleeds, the players [were] as big as my fingernails."

It didn't matter. Young Joe was entranced. "I knew right away hockey was what I wanted."

And so he worked at it: he practiced relentlessly, he focused on conditioning, and he developed what many consider one of the greatest wrist shots ever.

But that, of course, is just one of Sakic's claims to fame. The stats sheets spell out the rest.

In 1997–98, the 5' 11" center finished third on the Avalanche point roster, with 63. One of the finest playmakers in the league, Sakic was the NHL playoff assist leader the previous season. In early 1998, he also traveled to Nagano, Japan, as assistant captain of the Canadian men's hockey team in the Winter Olympics.

When Colorado took the Stanley Cup in 1996, it was Sakic who won the Conn Smythe, annually given to the most valuable player in the playoffs. And it was Sakic who made it into the NHL record books by scoring a staggering six game-winning goals in one postseason.

But high-level stats—and the accolades that accompany them—have been part of Sakic's hockey career ever since its beginning.

That was back in 1986, when Sakic was just 17. He joined the Swift Current Broncos in Saskatchewan, and he led the league with 133 points.

Midway through that first season, Sakic stepped on board a bus, along with the rest of his teammates, for the expected half-hour trip to nearby Regina for a game against the Pats. It was a trip that will forever be etched in Sakic's memory.

About five minutes into the trip, the bus skidded on a sheet of black ice and went out of control. It rolled and crashed into some signposts. When it was over, four players sitting in the rear of the bus were dead.

Sakic moved on like a player possessed after the

accident. His point tally with the Broncos climbed to 160 the following season. There would be 78 goals scored in 64 games, enough to earn him player of the year honors.

By the time he moved to the NHL—Sakic was the Quebec Nordiques' 2nd-round draft pick and 15th overall in the 1987 Entry Draft—he'd become a consummate professional. In three of his first five seasons, his point total was 100-plus.

But if Sakic was soaring, the Nordiques were not. In five of Sakic's seven seasons with the Quebec franchise, the Nordiques failed to make it to the postseason. In their two playoff years, they lasted a single round.

Sakic calls his final years in Quebec—the years before the Nordiques died and were reborn as the Avalanche—a time of "rebuilding." Yes, says Sakic, they were difficult, but that's as far as this diplomat will go. "Nothing against Quebec. It's a great hockey town."

By 1996, of course, the rebuilding was complete. The Cup confirmed that.

And Sakic was in the spotlight as he'd never been before—whether he wanted to be or not. The New York Rangers made a hugely publicized bid to sign Sakic as a restricted free agent. The Avs, however, weren't about to bid adieu to their captain, and matched the Rangers' whopping $21 million offer over three years, including an unusual $15-million signing bonus.

It's the kind of attention that could make you a little bit high on yourself.

But not if you're Joe Sakic. He's been on the front of *TV Guide*, of *Hockey News*, even the Denver phone book.

And he wonders what all the fuss is about.

#19 JOE SAKIC, Colorado Avalanche, center

YEAR	TEAM	LEA	REGULAR SEASON					PLAYOFFS				
			GP	G	A	TP	PIM	GP	G	A	TP	PIM
1986-87	Swift Current	WHL	72	60	73	133	31	4	0	1	1	0
	Cdn. National	.....	1	0	0	0	0	.....	.....	.....	.....	.....
1987-88	Swift Current	WHL	64	78	82	160	64	10	11	13	24	12
1988-89	Quebec	NHL	70	23	39	62	24	.....	.....	.....	.....	.....
1989-90	Quebec	NHL	80	39	63	102	27	.....	.....	.....	.....	.....
1990-91	Quebec	NHL	80	48	61	109	24	.....	.....	.....	.....	.....
1991-92	Quebec	NHL	69	29	65	94	20	.....	.....	.....	.....	.....
1992-93	Quebec	NHL	78	48	57	105	40	6	3	3	6	2
1993-94	Quebec	NHL	84	28	64	92	18	.....	.....	.....	.....	.....
1994-95	Quebec	NHL	47	19	43	62	30	6	4	1	5	0
1995-96	Colorado	NHL	82	51	69	120	44	22	18	16	34	14
1996-97	Colorado	NHL	65	22	52	74	34	17	8	17	25	14
1997-98	Colorado	NHL	64	27	36	63	50	6	2	3	5	6

Mats Sundin

Toronto Maple Leafs

There was never a time that hockey didn't figure in the life of Mats Sundin.

It was always there, not only for Mats, but also for his big brother, Patrick, and his kid brother, Per. Their father, a former junior goalie, had the boys take shots on him at the family home in Sweden.

Dad was also around to offer comfort when his talented middle boy arrived home distraught after losing a hockey game.

"When we'd lose a game, my whole world was coming apart," recalls Sundin, who was born in the community of Bromma. "I couldn't handle it."

Sundin has changed considerably since his boyhood days in Sweden. He's 27 now, stands 6' 4" and tips the scales at 225 pounds. And he lives in Toronto, an ocean away from the place where he grew up.

But Mats Sundin still values victory as much as he ever did. He may no longer cry when his Maple Leafs lose, but he certainly celebrates—along with all of Toronto—when they win.

"When you are winning, it is the best," says

"I may sometimes look like I'm so nice that I can't get mad," says Sundin. "But I can be a pain—for the other team."

Sundin. "You can't be in a better city. I am very happy there."

Sundin has been with the Leafs since 1994, when he was traded from the Quebec Nordiques, who had picked him up first overall in the 1989 NHL Entry Draft. Sundin was originally a winger, but the Leafs moved him to center after Doug Gilmour left for New Jersey. In the fall of 1997, he was named captain of the Leafs, becoming the first non-Canadian to earn that honor.

Leafs president and general manager Ken Dryden couldn't have imagined a better candidate for the job.

"You know what leadership is when you walk into a room and see four people sitting around one person," says Dryden. "That person that's being sat around is the leader. And this is Mats' time."

It's his time, indeed.

Sundin was by far the top point man for Toronto in 1997–98, scoring 33 goals and adding 41 assists for 74 points. He also earned the most points the previous two seasons, accumulating 83 in 1995–96 and 94 in 1996–97.

Sundin has made appearances in NHL All-Star games and was twice named to the Swedish League All-Star team. He represented his homeland at the 1998 Olympics in Nagano, Japan, and has taken part in four world championships.

The Leafs captain, like most European hockey players, grew up prizing Olympic gold more than glory in the NHL. Now, however, Sundin's perspective has changed.

"It would be great to win at the Olympics," he says, "but I would consider winning a Stanley Cup bigger. . . . Learning about the NHL, and learning how competitive the league is, and seeing you've got to be fortunate to get on a Stanley Cup–bound team, it's certainly a prize that's tougher to reach."

Hopes are high around Toronto that Sundin is the kind of player who'll help boost the performance of the Leafs, who failed to make it past the regular season in 1996–97 and 1997–1998.

Sundin is, after all, a gifted athlete, and perhaps

the most talented hockey player to wear a Maple Leafs jersey in a long time.

"He is an elite player," says the *Hockey Scouting Report*. "Sundin is a big skater who looks huge, as he uses an ultralong stick that gives him a broad wingspan. For a big man, he is an agile skater."

The *Report* says that Sundin, regarded by some as perhaps the most underrated player in the NHL, is also an athlete who is respected by his teammates and his coaches. In other words, he's a leader.

Former Leafs head coach Mike Murphy says the generally soft-spoken Sundin is the perfect candidate to lead the Leafs.

"Most leaders are quiet and they have resolved themselves to play well," says Murphy. "But when you do talk, you have to make sense and you have to say the right things. Not something that's popular, not something that's acceptable, but something that makes sense."

To Sundin, leadership occasionally means abandoning your good-natured visage and doing a little hollering.

"I may sometimes look like I'm so nice that I can't get mad," says Sundin. "But I can be a pain—for the other team."

He says he also won't hesitate to single out members of his own team, when necessary. "People make honest mistakes. But if you see a teammate floating around or not doing his job, I'm not afraid to tell

anyone or make sure they know. I can be that way."

Tough, talented, and committed to victory—that's what Mats Sundin is all about.

"This is such a great hockey city," he says of his new hometown. "The people in Toronto support the team even when it's losing. It would be great for the fans if we could give them a winner."

#13 MATS SUNDIN, Toronto Maple Leafs, center

| YEAR | TEAM | LEA | REGULAR SEASON | | | | | PLAYOFFS | | | | |
			GP	G	A	TP	PIM	GP	G	A	TP	PIM
1988-89	Nacka	Swe. 2	25	10	8	18	18	....	.....	.....	.....	.....
1989-90	Djurgarden	Swe.	34	10	8	18	16	8	7	0	7	4
1990-91	Quebec	NHL	80	23	36	59	58	.....	.....	.....	.....	.....
1991-92	Quebec	NHL	80	33	43	76	103	.....	.....	.....	.....	.....
1992-93	Quebec	NHL	80	47	67	114	96	6	3	1	4	6
1993-94	Quebec	NHL	84	32	53	85	60	.....	.....	.....	.....	.....
1994-95	Djurgarden	Swe.	12	7	2	9	14	.....	.....	.....	.....	.....
	Toronto	NHL	47	23	24	47	14	7	5	4	9	4
1995-96	Toronto	NHL	76	33	50	83	46	6	3	1	4	4
1996-97	Toronto	NHL	82	41	53	94	59	.....	.....	.....	.....	.....
1997-98	Toronto	NHL	82	33	41	74	49	.....	.....	.....	.....	.....

Doug Weight

Edmonton Oilers

Edmonton Oilers center Doug Weight grew up like most red-blooded Canadian boys. Most often with a hockey stick in his hand, skates on his feet, dreaming of scoring the winning goal in the Stanley Cup Finals. And then skating around the ice, hoisting the biggest trophy in professional sports. Except Doug Weight wasn't Canadian. His hockey dreams started south of the border, in Warren, Michigan.

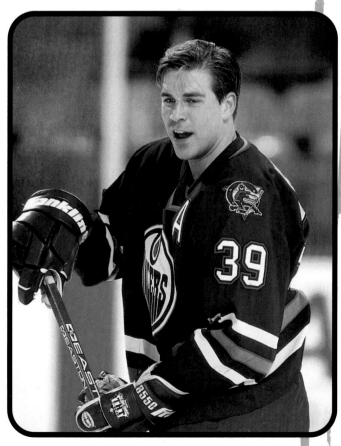

Like so many kids, Weight's hockey career began in the kitchen of his family's home. With a ping-pong ball and a little plastic Detroit Red Wings hockey stick, which never left his hand. "Whatever he did, he had that ping pong ball and stick," said Doug Weight Sr.

He's led the Oilers in scoring the last five seasons.

"I was an NHLer," Weight the Oiler recalls of those early days. "I would always try to shoot it upstairs on dad and I'd shoot my mom's shins. I was a terror." Besides an uncommon determination, a father saw a son with uncommon skill as well. "I thought Doug had a good chance to make it all along," Doug Sr. says. "We worked on his skill. It was just a question of size. I didn't know if he was going to be big enough and, of course,

there's the desire to take into consideration."

Being from Michigan, it was no surprise that the Wings were Weight's favorite team, and Detroit captain Steve Yzerman his favorite player. Weight would watch *Hockey Night in Canada* on weekends and loved following the play of his hockey hero, Yzerman.

Not surprisingly, Weight would become a play-making center who not only exhibited many of the same skills Yzerman possessed on the ice, but also much of the same, upstanding character the Wings captain has become known for off the ice too.

And so it is, that Weight has become involved with many charities in Edmonton. He and wife, Allison, also bought a skysuite at the Edmonton Coliseum for sufferers of cancer and their families. The suite is called Weight's World.

"When you talk to a little kid with cancer who says he wants to become a hockey player just like you, there's a perspective," says Weight. "It's fun to give something back. We're pro athletes, we're very lucky but some people aren't."

The Oilers were lucky too when a trade with the New York Rangers on March 17, 1993, brought Weight to Edmonton in exhange for Esa Tikkanen. Weight had been the Rangers second choice, 34th overall, in the 1990 Entry Draft. Weight had played college hockey for two seasons with the Lake Superior State Lakers of the Central Collegiate Hockey Association.

In his first NHL game, on October 3, 1991, Doug Weight showed he belonged, getting his first goal against then–Boston goalie Andy Moog. Since moving to Edmonton, Weight has emerged as a team leader, centering the club's top line. His best season was 1995–96 when he scored 25 goals and added an impressive 79 assists for a 104 point campaign. His numbers tailed off the last two seasons, as goal scoring totals around the league dropped in the face of tougher defensive systems by most teams. In 1996–97 he had 21 goals and 61 assists for 82 points, while this past season he had 26 goals and 44 assists for 70 points. He's led the Oilers in scoring the last five seasons.

Weight's numbers betray his obvious strong suit—playmaking. And like most great playmakers, Weight has excellent peripheral vision and can make passes well to either side. He has also earned a reputation as one of the best one-on-one players in the league.

Grittiness is another trait Weight has become known for, particularly after playing 10 playoff games for the Oilers in 1996–97 with a separated shoulder.

Every year in the league, Weight, 27, has just gotten better to where now he is on everyone's list as one of the premier centers in the NHL today.

"I love Edmonton, I love Canada, I love the people and the hockey is great," says Weight.

"I'm a proud Oiler."

#39 DOUG WEIGHT, Edmonton Oilers, center

| YEAR | TEAM | LEA | REGULAR SEASON | | | | | PLAYOFFS | | | | |
			GP	G	A	TP	PIM	GP	G	A	TP	PIM
1989-90	Lake Superior	CCHA	46	21	48	69	44	.....	.....	.....	.....	.....
1990-91	Lake Superior	CCHA	42	29	46	75	86	.....	.....	.....	.....	.....
	NY Rangers	NHL	.....	.....	.....	.....	.....	1	0	0	0	0
1991-92	NY Rangers	NHL	53	8	22	30	23	7	2	2	4	0
	Binghamton	AHL	9	3	14	17	2	4	1	4	5	6
1992-93	NY Rangers	NHL	65	15	25	40	55	.....	.....	.....	.....	.....
	Edmonton	NHL	13	2	6	8	10	.....	.....	.....	.....	.....
1993-94	Edmonton	NHL	84	24	50	74	47	.....	.....	.....	.....	.....
1994-95	Rosenheim	Ger.	8	2	3	5	18	.....	.....	.....	.....	.....
	Edmonton	NHL	48	7	33	40	69	.....	.....	.....	.....	.....
1995-96	Edmonton	NHL	82	25	79	104	95	.....	.....	.....	.....	.....
1996-97	Edmonton	NHL	80	21	61	82	80	12	3	8	11	8
1997-98	Edmonton	NHL	79	26	44	70	69	12	2	7	9	14

Alexei Yashin

Ottawa Senators

Alexei Yashin is a big man with a big heart. And in Ottawa, hometown of the franchise that Yashin has helped lift into the playoffs the last two seasons, he's nothing short of a hero.

Folks love the guy.

"They show their love for Alexei a lot more openly than they used to," says Yashin's agent, Mark Gandler.

No wonder. The Russian center did, after all, lead the Senators in goals and points in the last two seasons. He does, after all, have a genuine appreciation for his fans.

He did, after all, open up his wallet and donate some cash to Ottawa's National Arts Center in March, 1998. That's cash as in a cool $1 million.

When he made the donation, Yashin said he hoped the money would bring performers and artists from his Russian homeland to Canada's cap-

ital city, and also encourage more youth programs. He said his appreciation of the arts was because of his parents, who'd introduced him to dance and music as a young child.

The gesture did not go unnoticed.

Alexei Yashin is part hockey player, part philanthropist.

"People on the street have always recognized Alexei, but now they scream thank yous across the street to him," says Gandler.

At a ceremony at Ottawa's Corel Centre, in which a Senators jersey was presented to Gordie Howe, the applause for Yashin seemed louder than that for Howe. When Yashin made another public appearance, this one sponsored by a clothing company, hundreds of adoring fans waiting patiently for an opportunity to get an autograph.

And all over the Corel Centre, fans have erected placards reading: "Thanks a million, Yash!"

Alexei Yashin is part hockey player, part philanthropist.

The philanthropist part has been responsible for acts of kindness by Yashin. When the wife of a popular Canadian hockey commentator died, Yashin made a generous donation to the family's chosen charity. And after a 1997 car accident involving members of the Detroit Red Wings and a trainer, Yashin made a donation to support the trainer's family.

Yashin is a class act.

He's also a pretty good hockey player, good enough to have topped the Senators' point race in 1997–98, scoring 33 goals and adding 39 assists for 72 points. A year earlier, he also led the team in goals and points.

The 24-year-old Yashin, who hails from Sverdlovsk, Russia, is widely considered the best player on the Senators.

Dubbed the Russian Bear by broadcasters, Yashin is both big and strong—he's 6' 3" and weighs 225 pounds.

The *Hockey Scouting Report* describes Yashin—or Yash, as he's come to be known—as a player who may not be flashy, but who has a powerful shot and great stick-handling ability.

"Yashin's skills rank with any of the new guard of

players who have entered the NHL in the last three seasons," says the *Report*. "He has great hands and size. As he stickhandles in on the rush, he can put the puck through the legs of two or three defenders en route to the net."

In the past, some described Yashin as a player who was often brilliant, but who lacked consistency. But in 1996–97 he began to develop more of a presence in every game.

Yashin was the Senators' No. 1 pick—and second overall—in the 1992 NHL Entry Draft. A year later, he was a member of the Russian squad that won the World Hockey Championships. In 1998, he represented his homeland again, traveling to the Olympics in Nagano, Japan, and returning with a silver medal.

In Yashin's rookie year with the Senators, he finished up as the franchise's top scorer and represented his team at the NHL All-Star Game.

A contract dispute that stretched from the summer of 1994 until the end of 1995 saw Yashin miss 35 games and did little for his popularity. The Senators also struggled during that period, and the Corel Centre was less than full.

Things, however, have turned around. Yashin signed a new deal, the Senators became rejuvenated, and the fans began to holler louder than they ever had before.

"There was a lot of talk about me for a couple of years," says Yashin. "[But] I live my life and do the best I can do for the team."

Perhaps the biggest vote of confidence in Yashin came when he was designated assistant to captain Randy Cunneyworth in the fall of 1997.

"It's a responsibility for me to step it up and make something happen," Yashin said at the time. "That's what team leaders are. They are the groups of guys who make something happen in difficult situations and make the team play better."

If that, indeed, is what leaders do, then that's exactly what Alexei Yashin has done.

#19 ALEXEI YASHIN, Ottawa Senators, center

YEAR	TEAM	LEA	REGULAR SEASON					PLAYOFFS				
			GP	G	A	TP	PIM	GP	G	A	TP	PIM
1990-91	Sverdlovsk	USSR	26	2	1	3	10	.....	.....	.....	.....	.....
1991-92	Moscow D'amo	CIS	35	7	5	12	19	.....	.....	.....	.....	.....
1992-93	Moscow D'amo	CIS	27	10	12	22	18	10	7	3	10	18
1993-94	Ottawa	NHL	83	30	49	79	22	.....	.....	.....	.....	.....
1994-95	Las Vegas	IHL	24	15	20	35	32	.....	.....	.....	.....	.....
	Ottawa	NHL	47	21	23	44	20	.....	.....	.....	.....	.....
1995-96	CSKA	CIS	4	2	2	4	4	.....	.....	.....	.....	.....
	Ottawa	NHL	46	15	24	39	28	.....	.....	.....	.....	.....
1996-97	Ottawa	NHL	82	35	40	75	44	7	1	5	6	2
1997-98	Ottawa	NHL	82	33	39	72	24	11	5	3	8	8

Steve Yzerman

Detroit Red Wings

If ever there was a hockey player who deserves to wear the captain's insignia, it's Detroit's Steve Yzerman.

Yzerman has earned the honor — season after season. In the 1997–98 season, he led the Red Wings in scoring with 24 goals and 45 assists for 69 points. That moved the center up the ladder on both the NHL's all-time scoring list and all-time points list. By the end of the regular season, he'd accumulated 563 career goals, 3 goals ahead of Guy Lafleur and only 10 behind Mike Bossy. On the all-time points roster, he stood at 1,409 points, just 16 points behind Bryan Trottier, who sits in tenth place overall.

> "I said I just hoped he'd be paid to play hockey," recalls Steve's dad. "Geez, the price of sticks."

To be placed in the history books among the likes of Lafleur and Trottier is nothing short of thrilling for the 33–year-old native of Cranbrook, British Columbia. Growing up, Trottier was Yzerman's hockey hero. He even picked his number—19—because it belonged to Trottier.

"I don't consider myself an equal to those guys at all," says Yzerman. "I just think it is kind of neat from my perspective to see my name among them because these were the guys that I really idolized as a kid."

These days, the kids who lace up their skates at dawn and dream of careers in the NHL are not

thinking Bryan Trottier when they think of No. 19. They're thinking Steve Yzerman.

For years now, he's been a hero in his own right. Pretty amazing—especially considering that Ron and Jean Yzerman didn't even know hockey could be a career until Steve was around 15.

Sure, Ron always had a sense that Stephen—the third of his five children—had some talent with a hockey puck. But he says he honestly didn't think beyond that. "I think unless you're stupid, you don't say he's going to be in the National Hockey League," says Ron, who moved the family to Nepean, Ontario, an Ottawa suburb, when Steve was 10. "It's when scouts start approaching you and telling you what they see that you believe he might have a career in hockey."

Yzerman, who's captained the Wings for 12 of the 15 years he's been with the club, made his hockey debut when he was five. In no time, he was asked to play with kids twice his age.

One story has it that Yzerman and his brothers were so passionate about hockey they even convinced their babysitting grandmother once that they were allowed to play in the hall of their home. Grandma was even talked into joining the game.

Terry Hayden, a childhood friend of Steve's, played hockey with Yzerman for five years on Nepean's premier team. He remembers his teammate being consistently exceptional. "Steve always delivered," says Hayden. In the years they played together, their team lasted 143 games without a loss.

When Yzerman was just 16, he left home for Peterborough, Ontario, to play junior hockey. At 18, he was picked by the Red Wings in the entry draft. He was Detroit's first choice, and fourth overall. Ron Yzerman was with his son the day the Wings drafted him, and remembers speaking to club owner Mike Ilitch.

"I said I just hoped he'd be paid to play hockey," recalls Ron. "Geez, the price of sticks."

That was in 1983. And ever since, Yzerman has been making the Wings proud of their choice.

Yzerman's tenure with Detroit reached its pinnacle in 1997, when he captained the team to its first Stanley Cup victory since 1955.

But just as there are highs in hockey, so are there lows—and Yzerman experienced one of them in Nagano, Japan, at the 1998 Winter Olympics. He traveled to Nagano, a member of the Canadian hockey team, with visions of gold in his head, but the team returned with no medal at all.

"I was, when it ended, very disappointed," says Yzerman. "I figured that was my one chance."

A gold medal, he says, would have looked awfully pretty alongside a Stanley Cup.

"It would be a great experience or a great accomplishment at the end of your career to say that you played on winners on both of those." Still, the philosophical Yzerman says the Olympic experience was tremendous. He also says it re-energized his game.

"I'm just skating more and trying to accelerate," he says. "Going to the Olympics, the play was real high-tempo, fast-skating, and I tried to continue a higher tempo game when I got back."

Danny Gare, former Wings captain, and now an announcer for Buffalo, says Yzerman's style may have changed somewhat over the years, but he still contributes considerably to the game.

"I remember him as a rookie, all bright-eyed and bushy-tailed. Even though he's getting older, he continues to excel. When they need somebody to push, he's the guy they look to."

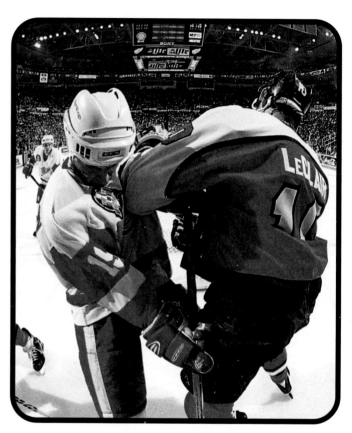

#19 STEVE YZERMAN, Detroit Red Wings, center												
			REGULAR SEASON					PLAYOFFS				
YEAR	TEAM	LEA	GP	G	A	TP	PIM	GP	G	A	TP	PIM
1981-82	Peterborough	OHL	58	21	43	64	65	6	0	1	1	16
1982-83	Peterborough	OHL	56	42	49	91	33	4	1	4	5	0
1983-84	Detroit	NHL	80	39	48	87	33	4	3	3	6	0
1984-85	Detroit	NHL	80	30	59	89	58	3	2	1	3	2
1985-86	Detroit	NHL	51	14	28	42	16	.....	.....	.....	.....	.....
1986-87	Detroit	NHL	80	31	59	90	43	16	5	13	18	8
1987-88	Detroit	NHL	64	50	52	102	44	3	1	3	4	6
1988-89	Detroit	NHL	80	65	90	155	61	6	5	5	10	2
1989-90	Detroit	NHL	79	62	65	127	79	.....	.....	.....	.....	.....
1990-91	Detroit	NHL	80	51	57	108	34	7	3	3	6	4
1991-92	Detroit	NHL	79	45	58	103	64	11	3	5	8	12
1992-93	Detroit	NHL	84	58	79	137	44	7	4	3	7	4
1993-94	Detroit	NHL	58	24	58	82	36	3	1	3	4	0
1994-95	Detroit	NHL	47	12	26	38	40	15	4	8	12	0
1995-96	Detroit	NHL	80	36	59	95	64	18	8	12	20	4
1996-97	Detroit	NHL	81	22	63	85	78	20	7	6	13	4
1997-98	Detroit	NHL	75	24	45	69	46	22	6	18	24	22

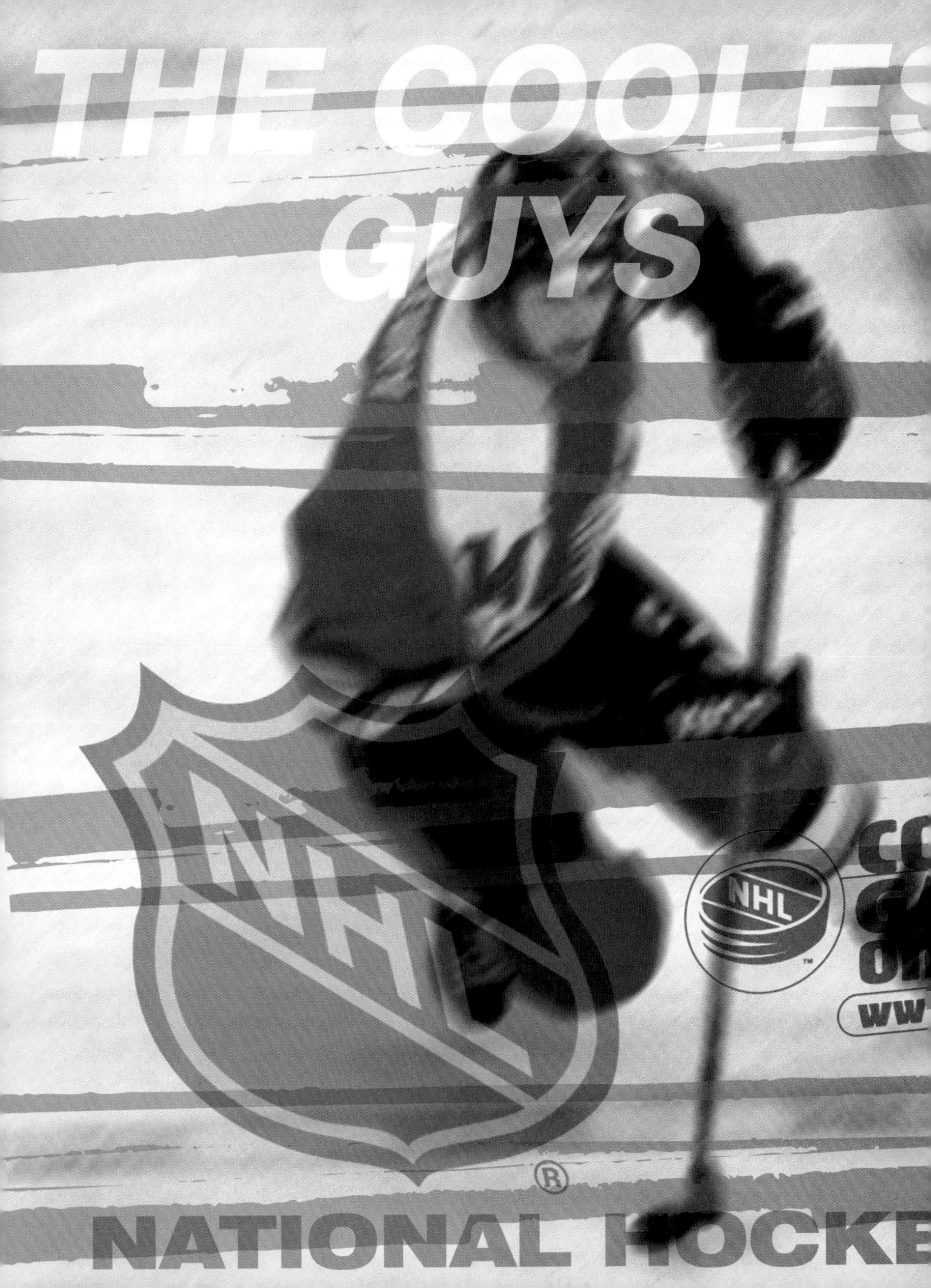
THE COOLES
GUYS
NHL
NHL
NATIONAL HOCKE

Wild Wingers

Drive Goalies Crazy

Peter Bondra

When Washington Capitals scoring sensation Peter Bondra hits a slump, he heads for his basement. Not to hide. But to look for an answer. "I go down into my basement and I have a tape of goals from the last seven years," Bondra explained this past season. "Basically, I watch them and try to learn what I did, how often I shot the puck on the net, if I go to the net or what kind of positions I score from.

"It's doing simple things and then all of a sudden you go into the game and it's going your way again."

It went Bondra's way a lot in 1997–98. And the year before that and the year before that. The Capitals better hope that the quiet right winger never loses that tape. Then again, he's scored enough goals to make dozens of goal-scoring tapes.

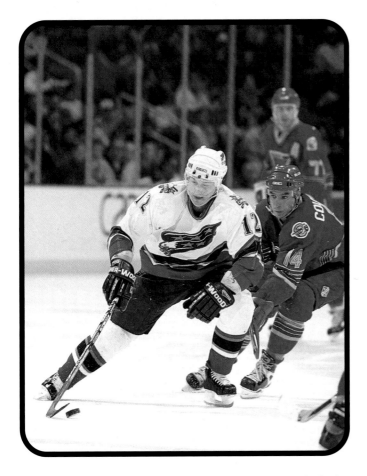

The 6'1", 200 pounder once again led the Capitals in offensive output this past season, scoring a league-leading 52 goals (tied with Anaheim's Teemu Selanne) and adding 26 assists for 78 points. As demure as his demeanor is ("I wouldn't say I'm shy, but I don't go up to strangers and say, 'Hi, I'm

Bondra has scored more goals in the NHL the last few seasons than anyone else.

Peter Bondra' either."), Bondra has been just as quiet about scoring more goals in the NHL the last few seasons than anyone else. That's right, Peter Bondra, not Jaromir Jagr or Selanne or Philadephia's John LeClair.

Since the beginning of the 1994–95 season, Bondra has scored 186 goals. His closest competitor over that period is LeClair with 178 goals. Jagr has 176 and Selanne, 165. This past year, Bondra also

made his fourth All-Star Game appearance in the last five years. Bondra, 30, may be the greatest player in the league who gets the least amount of credit for his amazing achievements. Not everyone, however, overlooks his impact on the sports scene in the capital of the United States.

Washington Times columnist Dan Daly concluded Bondra was the most important individual on any of the Washington major league teams. His competition included Chris Webber and Juwan Howard of the National Basketball Association's Wizards, Gus Frerotte and Michael Westbrook of the National Football League's Redskins, and— expanding the boundaries a touch—Robbie Alomar, Mike Mussina, and Brady Anderson of the Baltimore Orioles. "Hopefully things will change," Bondra said about his lack of recognition.

"Our team has to win a Stanley Cup. If you do that you will get more recognition as an individual."

While Bondra might not yet get the recognition he deserves, he is among that rarefied group of NHL players you would pay to watch. He is one of the fastest players in the league, with exceptional acceleration. Bondra often cuts in on the off-wing and shoots in stride. He will fire quickly or drive in close and deke and wrist a little shot behind a goalie.

While scouts were always aware of his speed, not many during the 1990 Entry Draft figured Bondra would one day rank as one of the league's top scorers. That's why the Capitals were able to draft him in the ninth round, 156th overall. He left VSZ Kosice of the Czechoslovakian league for the Capitals the same summer.

"Everything was new for me, like the smaller rinks and stuff like that," says the native of Luck, Ukraine. "But I talked to my new teammates, and they gave me some useful advice, especially [Czechoslovakian] Michal Pivonka, who already was here. He helped me both off and on the ice."

Bondra shared a line with Pivonka for his first few seasons, but Capitals coach Ron Wilson shook things up when he took over the team and paired the speedy sniper with center Adam Oates. It took awhile for the two to find each other on the ice, but now they're one of the most exciting tandems in the game.

"Peter has developed a real good chemistry with Adam," says Capitals assistant coach Tim Army. "Peter is a terrific one-on-one player, but I think the part of his game that's developed is the two-on-one part where you move the puck to Adam, then you get into an opening and you know Adam will then get the puck back to you. It's more than a give and go," Army explains. "It's more like how Gretzky and Kurri played, or Kariya and Selanne."

Left-winger Chris Simon says of Bondra: "He has a gift; he can score goals. A lot of guys can set up plays, a lot of guys can fight, but there's not that many guys around who can score goals." Like so many goal scorers, Bondra's points have come in streaks. He can break a six-game scoreless streak with four goals against Colorado. "Goal scorers are streaky," explains Wilson. "When they start feeling good about themselves they jump into holes. With Peter, he seems a lot more energized when things are going well. He has a lot more jump."

The Capitals realize how vital Bondra is to the team's success. His numbers don't lie. In the 1997–98 season, he led the NHL with 13 game-winning goals and accounted for 23.7 percent of his

team's goals. That's up from 21.5 the year before. Only Teemu Selanne, with 25.3 percent of his team's 205 goals, was better.

"My job is to score goals," Bondra says simply. And when he's not, he just heads to his basement to rediscover his touch.

#12 PETER BONDRA, Washington Capitals, right wing

| YEAR | TEAM | LEA | REGULAR SEASON | | | | | PLAYOFFS | | | | |
			GP	G	A	TP	PIM	GP	G	A	TP	PIM
1986-87	VSZ Kosice	Czech.	32	4	5	9	24	.....	.....	.....	.....	.....
1987-88	VSZ Kosice	Czech.	45	27	11	38	20	.....	.....	.....	.....	.....
1988-89	VSZ Kosice	Czech.	40	30	10	40	20	.....	.....	.....	.....	.....
1989-90	VSZ Kosice	Czech.	49	36	19	55	.....	.....	.....	.....	.....	.....
1990-91	Washington	NHL	54	12	16	28	47	4	0	1	1	2
1991-92	Washington	NHL	71	28	28	56	42	7	6	2	8	4
1992-93	Washington	NHL	83	37	48	85	70	6	0	6	6	0
1993-94	Washington	NHL	69	24	19	43	40	9	2	4	6	4
1994-95	Kosice	Slov.	2	1	0	1	0	.....	.....	.....	.....	.....
	Washington	NHL	47	34	9	43	24	7	5	3	8	10
1995-96	Detroit	IHL	7	8	1	9	0	.....	.....	.....	.....	.....
	Washington	NHL	67	52	28	80	40	6	3	2	5	8
1996-97	Washington	NHL	77	46	31	77	72	.....	.....	.....	.....	1
1997-98	Washington	NHL	76	52	26	78	44	17	7	5	12	12

Pavel Bure

Vancouver Canucks

He is flash, he is lightning, he is electricity on ice.

He is Pavel Bure, and he is like no other hockey player the National Hockey League has ever seen before.

"Pavel is incredible."

It's the highest of compliments, especially considering where it's coming from: six-time Stanley Cup winner Mark Messier.

Messier, Bure's line-mate on the Vancouver Canucks, has skated with some of the best hockey players in history. But in Bure, the boyish-looking 27-year-old from Moscow, Messier sees something rare, something bright, something particularly exciting.

"He is as good a player as there is in the world right now," says the Canucks captain. "He's been our best player hands down."

No question about that. For seven years now, he's been lifting the Canucks fans out of their seats, dazzling them night after night with his almost otherworldly speed and pizzazz. In 1997–98 Bure recorded 51 goals and 39 assists for 90 points. In the league's overall point race, he ended up tied with Wayne Gretzky for third place.

He is flash, he is lightning, he is electricity on ice.

Points speak volumes, but it's not the numbers race that truly distinguishes Pavel Bure. It's the way he moves.

Pat Burns, who coached the Toronto Maple Leafs in 1994, the year they lost to Vancouver in the

Western Conference Finals, told his players at the time to be particularly wary of the right winger they called the Russian Rocket. "I said, 'See that face. Remember it in your dreams—and stop him.' "

That's no small assignment. Former Canuck Esa Tikkanen, who now plays for the Washington Capitals, says Bure moves at turbospeed.

"He really is a rocket," says Tikkanen. "You've got to keep close to him at all times. You can't let him out of your sight for a second because he will shift into one of those higher gears and leave you standing still, wondering what happened."

Speed on the straightaway is impressive enough, but Bure also has an uncanny ability to stop on a dime, change direction, then blast off again— moves other players have tried, without success, to duplicate.

"I'd trip myself up if I tried some of those moves," says Wayne Gretzky. "The amazing thing about Pavel is he makes those moves at high speed in game situations. That's the difference."

Bure laced up his first skates—a pair of women's figure skates worth about $5—when he was six. His father, Vladimir, an accomplished swimmer who competed for the Soviet Union in three Olympics, had tried to sell Pavel on the idea of becoming a competitive swimmer, but had no luck at all. Pavel's dreams were centered on an ice rink, not a swimming pool.

"He would come into the house after hours of hockey practice," recalls Vladimir, who coached Bure as a youngster and continued on as his personal trainer after he joined the Canucks. "He would eat, change into his clothes, and then play hockey with the kids in our apartment."

Bure was enrolled in the Red Army hockey program and became an immediate force in youth, and then junior, hockey. But in 1988–89, his audience became international: that was when he participated in the World Junior Championships in Alaska and played on an unstoppable line with Sergei Fedorov and Alexander Mogilny. In that series, he scored eight goals and added six assists and was named top forward of the tournament.

Bure, who later played for two other medal-winning Soviet junior teams, was then picked up by the Canucks in the NHL's 1989 Entry Draft. And Vancouver fans were about to be treated to something they'd never witnessed before.

In 1991–92 Bure added another trophy to his collection: the Calder, handed out annually to the league's top rookie. The next season, he recorded an amazing 110 points. The following year, 107.

Bure's tenure with the Canucks, however, hasn't been without its disappointments. In the seasons that followed Vancouver's run-up to the 1994 Stanley Cup Finals, Bure was plagued with a knee injury, then neck problems. He ceased to be a contender, and so, it seemed, did the Canucks.

Rockets, however, are tough to extinguish. Bure recovered from his injuries in a big way. He re-emerged as a top goal-scorer, not only for Vancouver, but also for the Russian Olympic team.

Bure traveled to Nagano, Japan, in early 1998 as a member of Team Russia. He proved to be the team's engine, scoring nine goals in six games, including five in one semifinal game against Finland. He was named the tournament's top forward.

Bure could recall playing such a game just once before in his life. He was 12 when he scored nine

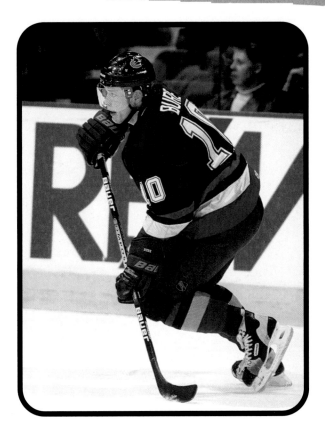

goals in a 30-0 game played in Moscow.

"That is a performance that is going to be in Olympic history," laughed Valeri Bure, Pavel's younger brother and teammate on Team Russia, which returned with Olympic silver.

It was, however, the kind of performance you'd expect from a guy whose coach has labeled him a superstar. Pavel Bure will definitely be in the history books. And his story will be anything but dull.

#10 PAVEL BURE, Vancouver Canucks, right wing

YEAR	TEAM	LEA	REGULAR SEASON					PLAYOFFS				
			GP	G	A	TP	PIM	GP	G	A	TP	PIM
1987-88	CSKA	USSR	5	1	1	2	0	.....	.....	.....	.....	.....
1988-89	CSKA	USSR	32	17	9	26	8	.....	.....	.....	.....	.....
1989-90	CSKA	USSR	46	14	10	24	20	.....	.....	.....	.....	.....
1990-91	CSKA	USSR	44	35	11	46	24	.....	.....	.....	.....	.....
1991-92	Vancouver	NHL	65	34	26	60	30	13	6	4	10	14
1992-93	Vancouver	NHL	83	60	50	110	69	12	5	7	12	8
1993-94	Vancouver	NHL	76	60	47	107	86	24	16	15	31	40
1994-95	Landshut	Ger.	1	3	0	3	2	.....	.....	.....	.....	.....
	Spartak	CIS	1	2	0	2	2	.....	.....	.....	.....	.....
	Vancouver	NHL	44	20	23	43	47	11	7	6	13	10
1995-96	Vancouver	NHL	15	6	7	13	8	.....	.....	.....	.....	.....
1996-97	Vancouver	NHL	63	23	32	55	40	.....	.....	.....	.....	.....
1997-98	Vancouver	NHL	82	51	39	90	48	.....	.....	.....	.....	.....

Theoren Fleury

Calgary Flames

They call him feisty. They call him gritty. Some even call him obnoxious. Meet him in combat on a hockey rink, and Theoren Fleury can be nothing short of a pest.

"He gets under your skin," one-time Edmonton Oiler Jeff Beukeboom said of the Calgary Flames right winger. "He's mouthy. He's trying to get you off your game." At 5' 6" and 170 pounds, Fleury may be the smallest player in the National Hockey League, but there's nothing timid about his style.

"Unable to find anyone his own size, Fleury picks on players 30 to 50 pounds heavier and half a foot taller," *Sports Illustrated* once said of Fleury. "He slashes at their calves, digs his elbows into their ribs and snarls insults, both generic and personal, at their psyches. "And as agitated opponents exhaust

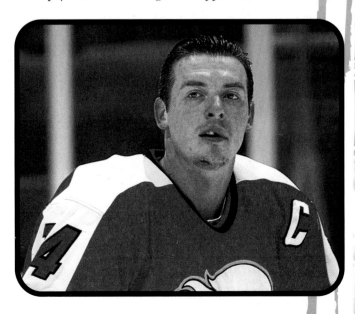

themselves chasing him, Fleury adds the ultimate insult: he streaks off to score or set up a goal."

If Fleury was always one of the shortest guys on the team, he was also one of the fastest. His skating and passing skills are exceptional, and he demonstrates both a fearlessness and a determination that constantly amaze onlookers. "He's like a sparkplug," says former Calgary winger Sandy McCarthy. "An engine needs a sparkplug to get started . . . He's in everybody's face. He puts the puck in the net."

> ## "I've proven that size is not a factor in how I play. Just watch me."

The Calgary captain, often described as the heart and soul of the Flames, was born in Oxbow, Saskatchewan, and grew up playing hockey on the ponds outside Russell, Manitoba. When he was 16, he went to Moose Jaw, Saskatchewan, to play junior hockey. He weighed 140 pounds at the time, and often found himself up against players 30 pounds heavier.

"I wondered what I was getting myself into," Fleury recalls. "So I started to play that aggressive style." It worked—just ask Detroit's Steve Yzerman, who teamed up with Fleury in the 1996 World Cup of Hockey.

"As an opponent, you hate to play against him because he's so tenacious," says Yzerman. "He stirs things up. If there's a skirmish, he's always there and right in the middle of it."

In three of Fleury's four years in Moose Jaw, he racked up more than 100 points. In 1988, he captained the Canadian team that won gold at the World Junior Championships, and the same season he was named Junior Player-of-the-Year by *The Hockey News*.

Fleury started out the 1988–89 season in Salt Lake, with the IHL, where he scored 74 points in just 40 games. He finished that season in Calgary, having been drafted eighth by the Flames in the 1987 NHL Entry Draft. Fleury says that first season with Calgary, the one in which the Flames won the Stanley Cup, goes down as his fondest hockey moment.

Fleury, who's 30, can't remember a day when he didn't dream of playing professional hockey. Nor can he recall a time when people didn't tell him he was too small to see that dream come true. "Even the girls were taller than me," says Fleury. "I was always the smallest guy."

Naturally, the comments about size quickly became annoying for Fleury, who wanted to prove that skill—and not height—is the important thing in hockey. "I want to get rid of the small label," says Fleury. "I've never played small, and I'm sick of answering questions about my height."

The irony, however, is that height didn't prevent Fleury from making the NHL. If anything, it helped get him there.

"I've always been driven by the height factor. Every time I step on the ice I want to make a statement: I am not small. Now it's the only way I know how to play, and it's what has kept me in the league."

That, of course, and his knack for putting a puck in the net. In 1997–98 Fleury celebrated his tenth year with the Flames by leading the club in points, scoring 27 goals and adding 51 assists for 78 points. Fleury, who averages almost 25 minutes of ice time per game, was one of only two Flames to play in every regular season game. It was the fourth consecutive season he'd led the Flames in goals, points, and shots. The speedy forward has played in numerous NHL All-Star Games, and in early 1998 traveled to

Nagano, Japan, with the Canadian Olympic hockey team, where he recorded four points in six games.

"We, as an organization, couldn't be more proud of what he has done," said Flames General Manager Al Coates, back when Fleury was named to Team Canada. "This city, his family, all of you should be proud."

Fleury, who now ranks as the Flames all-time leading goal scorer, hasn't done badly for a kid who was sometimes told he'd never make it to the big time. "I've proven that size is not a factor in how I play," Fleury said a couple of years back. "Just watch me." We have. And he's absolutely right.

#14 THEOREN FLEURY, Calgary Flames, right wing

YEAR	TEAM	LEA	REGULAR SEASON					PLAYOFFS				
			GP	G	A	TP	PIM	GP	G	A	TP	PIM
1984-85	Moose Jaw	WHL	71	29	46	75	82	.....	.....	.....	.....	.....
1985-86	Moose Jaw	WHL	72	43	65	108	124	.....	.....	.....	.....	.....
1986-87	Moose Jaw	WHL	66	61	68	129	110	9	7	9	16	34
1987-88	Moose Jaw	WHL	65	68	92	160	235	.....	.....	.....	.....	.....
	Salt Lake	IHL	2	3	4	7	7	8	11	5	16	16
1988-89	Salt Lake	IHL	40	37	37	74	81	.....	.....	.....	.....	.....
	Calgary	NHL	36	14	20	34	46	22	5	6	11	24
1989-90	Calgary	NHL	80	31	35	66	157	6	2	3	5	10
1990-91	Calgary	NHL	79	51	53	104	136	7	2	5	7	14
1991-92	Calgary	NHL	80	33	40	73	133	.....	.....	.....	.....	.....
1992-93	Calgary	NHL	83	34	66	100	88	6	5	7	12	27
1993-94	Calgary	NHL	83	40	45	85	186	7	6	4	10	5
1994-95	Tappara	Fin.	10	8	9	17	22	.....	.....	.....	.....	.....
	Calgary	NHL	47	29	29	58	112	7	7	7	14	2
1995-96	Calgary	NHL	80	46	50	96	112	4	2	1	3	14
1996-97	Calgary	NHL	81	29	38	67	104	.....	.....	.....	.....	.....
1997-98	Calgary	NHL	82	27	51	78	197	.....	.....	.....	.....	.....

Jaromir Jagr

Pittsburgh Penguins

The hair is his trademark, the long black curls that spill from the back of his helmet as he does battle on the ice. And recently, he added a salute to punctuate every goal he scores.

But there's more, of course, that characterizes Pittsburgh's Jaromir Jagr. Take speed. Take strength, or size, or skating ability. Or an unbelievable ability to hang on to a hockey puck.

There's more to Jaromir Jagr than a wave and flowing locks. An awful lot more.

"He's smart, he's a good skater, and most important in my opinion, he has great size and knows how to use it," says Wayne Gretzky. "He's the kind of guy who only comes along once in a while."

No question he's big: Jagr stands 6' 2" and weighs 228 pounds. No question, either, about his hockey smarts.

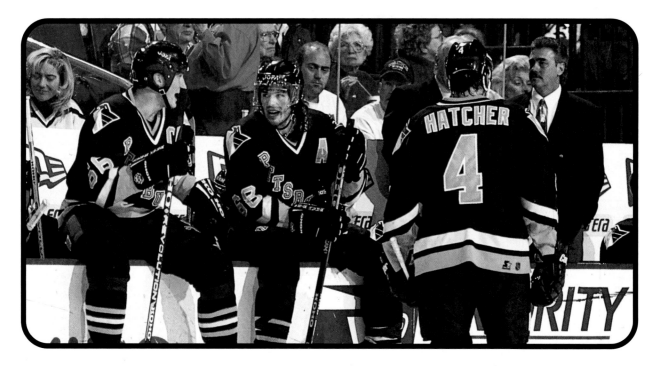

"Jaromir can play a clever game, and he can play a powerful game," says Penguins coach Kevin Constantine about his 26-year-old star right winger.

Anyone who's spent anytime examining Jagr's game—someone, for instance, like Penguins scout Greg Malone—knows there's one thing that seems to set the player apart from the rest. He sticks to the puck like a magnet.

What Jagr wants is simple: for "all the goals to be beautiful goals."

"The one thing that intrigued me the most was that he was so strong with the puck," says Malone, who's been enthralled with Jagr since seeing him at the world junior tournament in Finland in 1990. "Even though he was a young kid, when he got the puck and went wide with it or came out of the corners, no one could take the puck away from him.

"He was doing that at the age of 18 . . . and you don't see a lot of 18-year-olds play at that skill level."

The Penguins were impressed, not only with Jagr's skating and stickhandling, but also with his attitude.

"The one thing we liked when we talked to him before the draft," says Malone, "was that he obviously wanted to be the best player."

So taken were the Penguins with Jagr that they picked him first in the 1990 NHL Entry Draft. And all of a sudden, the hockey player from Kladno in the Czech Republic, a kid who'd grown up dreaming of freedom and who carried a picture of President Ronald Reagan in his schoolbook, was on his way to the United States.

Jagr gained his freedom, but remained fiercely proud of his homeland. He chose his number— 68—because that was the year of the Prague Spring insurgency, a time of temporary social reform that was quelled when Soviet tanks rolled into Prague, and into Wenceslas Square.

Ironically, Wenceslas Square was also the meeting place in 1998 for between 50,000 and 100,000 people who gathered on an unforgettable Sunday night to watch the Czech Republic's hockey team beat Russia 1-0 in the Nagano Olympics gold-medal round.

Representing the Czech Republic at the Olympics was a huge honor for Jagr, but it will go down as just one of many career highlights.

There were, of course, Pittsburgh's back-to-back

Stanley Cup victories in 1991 and 1992, Jagr's first two years with the Penguins. There was the Art Ross scoring title in 1994–95, and there have been numerous trips to NHL All-Star Games.

In 1997–98, the power forward was the top point man in the league, scoring 35 goals and adding 67 assists for 102 points. A season earlier, he accumulated just 7 points less, but in 1995–96—Jagr's blockbuster year—he scored a remarkable 62 goals, and assisted on 87 others for an impressive 149 points.

Jagr has, says one hockey observer, now succeeded superstar Mario Lemieux as the centerpiece of the Penguins franchise. Interesting—especially considering Lemieux has been Jagr's role model and idol ever since the two met in 1990.

Gretzky points to Jagr as one of the three best players in the NHL, the others being Colorado's Peter Forsberg and Philadelphia's Eric Lindros.

But Jagr, it seems, is not keen to spend his time pondering the most-valuable-player assessments. He'd rather do his job—work hard at practice, where he's usually the last guy off the ice, and work hard in game situations.

What Jagr wants is simple: for "all the goals to be beautiful goals."

"That's what you want to do, score good-looking goals and build up confidence for the next one you score," says Jagr.

"For me, the game is just a fun game. Being the MVP is not my goal. I just want to show some moves, have some fun. That's what it's about."

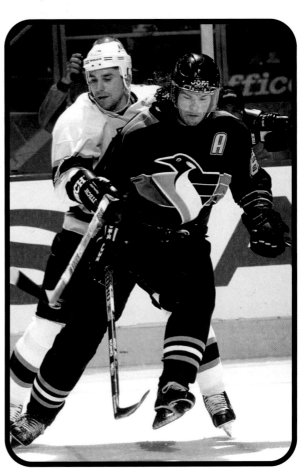

#68	JAROMIR JAGR, Pittsburgh Penguins, right wing											
			REGULAR SEASON					**PLAYOFFS**				
YEAR	TEAM	LEA	GP	G	A	TP	PIM	GP	G	A	TP	PIM
1988-89	Kladno	Czech.	39	8	10	18	4	.....	.....	.....	.....	.....
1989-90	Kladno	Czech.	51	30	29	59	.....	.....	.....	.....	.....	.....
1990-91	Pittsburgh	NHL	80	27	30	57	42	24	3	10	13	6
1991-92	Pittsburgh	NHL	70	32	37	69	34	21	11	13	24	6
1992-93	Pittsburgh	NHL	81	34	60	94	61	12	5	4	9	23
1993-94	Pittsburgh	NHL	80	32	67	99	61	6	2	4	6	16
1994-95	Kladno	Czech.	11	8	14	22	10	.....	.....	.....	.....	.....
	Bolzano	Euro.	5	8	8	16	4	.....	.....	.....	.....	.....
	Bolzano	Italy	1	0	0	0	0	.....	.....	.....	.....	.....
	Schalke	Ger. 2	1	1	10	11	0	.....	.....	.....	.....	.....
	Pittsburgh	NHL	48	32	38	70	37	12	10	5	15	6
1995-96	Pittsburgh	NHL	82	62	87	149	96	18	11	12	23	18
1996-97	Pittsburgh	NHL	63	47	48	95	40	5	4	4	8	4
1997-98	Pittsburgh	NHL	77	35	67	102	64	6	4	5	9	2

Paul Kariya

Mighty Ducks of Anaheim

Study Paul Kariya long enough and something starts to become apparent. This is not simply a hockey player with physical power. This one has brainpower too.

The 23-year-old captain of the Mighty Ducks of Anaheim possesses the best of both worlds. He can skate like the wind, but he can also plot some of the best moves ever seen on a hockey rink.

"Kariya is smart, some would say cerebral," says the *Hockey Scouting Report*. "He is a magician with the puck and can make a play when it looks as if there are no possible options."

"He is a magician with the puck and can make a play when it looks as if there are no possible options."

The mightiest Duck may not be big by NHL standards—he stands 5'11" and weighs 180 pounds—but he's definitely a powerhouse.

"Kariya may be the best skater in the NHL," says the *Report*. "He is so smooth and fluid his movements appear effortless. He's also explosive, with a good change of direction, and he can turn a defender inside out on a one-on-one rush."

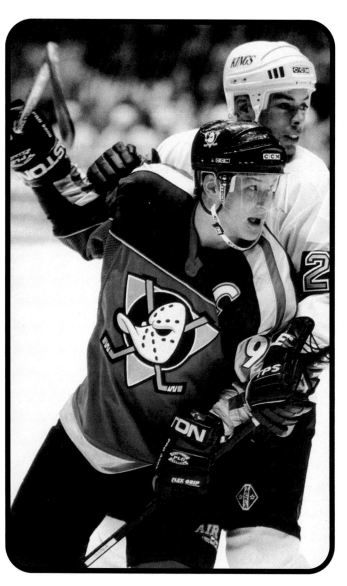

No wonder Anaheim snagged him in the first round of the 1993 NHL Entry Draft. It recognized a prize when it saw one.

Kariya, a left winger who was born in Vancouver, British Columbia, had accumulated a sterling resume before heading to California.

He'd been named Canadian Junior A Player of the Year in 1992, after scoring 46 goals and adding 86 assists for 132 points in just 40 games in Penticton, B.C. He'd twice been named the B.C. Junior Hockey League's Most Valuable Player. And he'd also been part of the Canadian gold medal–winning team at the 1992–93 World Junior Championships in Gavle, Sweden.

Oh yes, he'd also made it to the Dean's List when he was studying at the University of Maine, where he racked up 100 points in 39 college games, led the Black Bears to the national championship, and was the first freshman to win the Hobey Baker Award as top U.S. college hockey player.

Kariya, the Ducks observed, was something else indeed.

The oldest son of schoolteachers, Kariya grew up dreaming about hockey and thinking about Wayne Gretzky. And early on, he began to recognize that brainpower has a role to play in sports.

"I got into visualization early," he says. "I think the mind is the most important part of all sports. Where I lived in Vancouver, we didn't get ice time all that much, so I'd watch tapes and think about what I was going to do . . . You watch and you think. You learn by osmosis."

It took Kariya no time to start turning heads after moving to Anaheim.

In 1996–97, the third season he was with the Ducks, Kariya was voted a First Team NHL All-Star at left wing by the Professional Hockey Writers Association. He won the Lady Byng Trophy for the second year for being the player who exhibited the most sportsmanship "combined with a high standard of playing ability." He finished second in the balloting for the Hart Memorial

Trophy—for MVP—and ranked among the league leaders in goals, assists, and shots.

In 1994–95, the season in which he was a finalist for the Calder Memorial Trophy for outstanding league rookie, he was the leading scorer in Team Canada's ride to gold at the World Championships.

In Anaheim, hockey watchers noticed that Kariya was at his best when working alongside the Finnish Flash, teammate Teemu Selanne. They were, thought the Ducks, like a younger version of Mario Lemieux and Jaromir Jagr.

"We play really well together," Kariya said not long ago. "I wouldn't want to play with anybody else."

The pair may be potent, but they're also modest.

Ask Selanne who's best and he replies: "I think Paul has the greatest shot I've ever seen. He's an unbelievable passer too."

Ask Kariya and he's equally humble. "Teemu is a better pure scorer. I need 10 or 12 chances and he needs one to get one goal."

Kariya traveled to Lillehammer in 1994 to help the Canadian team take Olympic silver, and it was his dream to make a return trip to the Olympics in Nagano, Japan, in early 1998. But on February 1, a cross-check by Gary Suter of the Chicago Blackhawks put an end to those dreams. Kariya was sidelined with a concussion, which also kept him off the Ducks' roster for the remainder of the season. As he concentrated on rehabilitation, the

hockey world was hoping that the interruption in play would be short-lived.

After all, someone like Paul Kariya doesn't come along every day. He is, says L.A. defenseman Rob Blake, "one of the best players in the world."

#9 PAUL KARIYA, Mighty Ducks of Anaheim, left wing

YEAR	TEAM	LEA	REGULAR SEASON					PLAYOFFS				
			GP	G	A	TP	PIM	GP	G	A	TP	PIM
1992-93	U. of Maine	H.E.	36	24	69	93	12	3	1	6	7	0
1993-94	U. of Maine	H.E.	12	8	16	24	4	.....	.....	.....	.....	.....
	Cdn. National	.....	23	7	34	41	2	.....	.....	.....	.....	.....
	Cdn. Olympic	.....	8	3	4	7	2	.....	.....	.....	.....	.....
1994-95	Anaheim	NHL	47	18	21	39	4	.....	.....	.....	.....	.....
1995-96	Anaheim	NHL	82	50	58	108	20	.....	.....	.....	.....	.....
1996-97	Anaheim	NHL	69	44	55	99	6	11	7	6	13	4
1997-98	Anaheim	NHL	22	17	14	31	23	.....	.....	.....	.....	.....

Teemu Selanne

Mighty Ducks of Anaheim

Most of us are familiar with his nicknames: The Finnish Flash, The Flying Finn, Teddy Flash. Teddy Flash?

OK, that's one most hockey watchers haven't connected to Anaheim's Teemu Selanne. But it was what Selanne called himself, back in the days when he was a Winnipeg Jet.

The right winger, forever obsessed with speed, decided he wanted to try out auto racing. Afraid the Jets would object to such a dangerous activity, Selanne entered the 24-hour rallies under a pseudonym—Teddy Flash.

Selanne's never been interested in traveling in the slow lane. When he was a teenager growing up in Helsinki, he was fond of zipping across stretches of frozen ice on skates or skis, by hanging on to a tow rope being pulled by a speeding car.

Today, Selanne is still going full tilt—even without the car.

"Selanne has Porsche turbo speed," says the *Hockey Scouting Report*. "He gets down low and then simply explodes past defensemen, even when he starts from a standstill. . . . Acceleration, balance, change of gears, it's all there."

> ## "Selanne has Porsche turbo speed," says the *Hockey Scouting Report*.

So, too, is the ability to score goals. In 1997–98—the year in which Selanne's powerhouse partner, Paul Kariya, was out for half the season with a concussion—Selanne scored 52 goals and added 34 assists to lead the Mighty Ducks in points, with 86. Selanne was also a Hart finalist.

But then, scoring goals has always been what Selanne is all about. The 28-year-old astounded the NHL in his first season.

Back in 1992–93, Selanne scored 76 goals and added 56 assists for 132 points, shattering Mike Bossy's record of 53 goals by a rookie. Selanne, who'd grown up idolizing the likes of Guy Lafleur, Jari Kurri, and Wayne Gretzky, was naturally awarded the Calder Memorial Trophy for NHL Rookie-of-the-Year.

He's been on NHL All-Star teams and has represented his country on several Finnish national teams, including ones which have participated in the World Junior Championships, the World Championships, and the World Cup. Selanne has also made two trips to the Olympics on Finland's behalf: in 1992 in Albertville, France, and in 1998 in Nagano, Japan.

Those are pretty remarkable credentials for someone who started out as a kindergarten teacher. Selanne, who taught for three years in Finland, says he loves working with children and would have been a teacher's aid if he hadn't been a hockey player.

Folks who know Selanne describe him as a guy who's as good-natured off the ice as he is competitive on it.

"I'd say he's sort of a cross between a regular modern-day guy and a flower child," says former

Ducks defenseman Bobby Dollas. "He's a great hockey player, but he doesn't have a care in the world. When things are going bad, he's just so even-keeled that I'm sure it angers some guys."

Washington assistant Tim Army, who used to be with the Mighty Ducks, agrees that Selanne is as happy-go-lucky as they come.

"He just puts a smile on your face," says Army. "I've seen him stop the bus. He'll see some boys and girls with his jersey on and he'll get off the bus and sign autographs and talk to them."

It was in 1996 that Selanne was picked up by the Ducks from Winnipeg with the rights to Marc Chouinard, in exchange for Chad Kilger and Oleg Tverdovsky.

His exceptional talent became immediately recognized in Anaheim. He could move like a bolt of lightning, he could pass the puck with unbelievable accuracy, and he could shoot it like a rocket. Together with Kariya, Selanne became an opponent's worst nightmare.

"He plays off Kariya's puck control and exquisite lead passes," says the *Hockey Scouting Report*. "So often these two players will simply 'alley oop' to the other with perfect timing, so that they receive the puck in full stride."

In 1997, Selanne was a finalist for the Lady Byng Trophy, but was edged out by Kariya. It was the first time two players from the same team had been nominated for the Lady Byng in the same season.

"He's a very talented player," says one-time Ducks defenseman J. J. Daigneault of Selanne. "He always does something in the course of a game that raises eyebrows . . . He's very gifted, but he's also a hard worker."

Selanne may have attracted a reputation as a blur on ice, but there's more to this guy than sport. He supports children's charities. He teaches hockey school. He collects antique cars, likes to fish and jog, and enjoys his hand at card tricks. He works magic, it seems, both on and off the ice.

#8 TEEMU SELANNE, Mighty Ducks of Anaheim, right wing

			REGULAR SEASON					PLAYOFFS				
YEAR	TEAM	LEA	GP	G	A	TP	PIM	GP	G	A	TP	PIM
1987-88	Jokerit	Fin. Jr.	33	43	23	66	18	5	4	3	7	2
	Jokerit	Fin. 2	5	1	1	2	0	.....	.....	.....	.....	.....
1988-89	Jokerit	Fin. 2	34	35	33	68	12	5	7	3	10	4
1989-90	Jokerit	Fin.	11	4	8	12	0	.....	.....	.....	.....	.....
1990-91	Jokerit	Fin.	42	33	25	58	12	.....	.....	.....	.....	.....
1991-92	Jokerit	Fin.	44	39	23	62	20	10	10	7	17	18
1992-93	Winnipeg	NHL	84	76	56	132	45	6	4	2	6	2
1993-94	Winnipeg	NHL	51	25	29	54	22	.....	.....	.....	.....	.....
1994-95	Jokerit	Fin.	20	7	12	19	6	.....	.....	.....	.....	.....
	Winnipeg	NHL	45	22	26	48	2	.....	.....	.....	.....	.....
1995-96	Winnipeg	NHL	51	24	48	78	18	.....	.....	.....	.....	.....
	Anaheim	NHL	28	16	20	36	4	.....	.....	.....	.....	.....
1996-97	Anaheim	NHL	78	51	58	109	34	11	7	3	10	4
1997-98	Anaheim	NHL	73	52	34	86	30	.....	.....	.....	.....	.....

Zigmund Palffy

New York Islanders

First you notice the name. The unusual first one. Then you notice his play, unique in its own way too. Uniquely talented. Yes, Ziggy Palffy has got game and a great name. The quiet, shy kid from Skalica, Slovakia, has emerged as one of the NHL's finest goal-scorers and is the offensive centerpiece of a young team the New York Islanders hope soon matures into a Stanley Cup contender.

"Ziggy has always had trouble carrying the mantle of the team's best player, but it's unavoidable," says Islanders GM Mike Milbury. "When you drop the puck he's an excellent competitor."

Is he ever.

Palffy, 26, who prefers his formal first name Zigmund, was selected by New York in the second round, 26th overall, of the 1991 Entry Draft. While Palffy was a standout in the Czech league, there were questions about whether or not he could make the transition to the rough and tumble world of the NHL. Especially at his size. He was 5'10" and 183 pounds and played a finesse, European-style game, not a rugged, North American version.

When Palffy is on, he seems almost to dance on the ice.

Palffy broke in with the Islanders in the 1993–94 season, but when he was shipped back down to the minors, he was so homesick he went back to Slovakia. He returned the following season, playing 33 games and getting 10 goals and 7 assists for 17 points. The first couple of seasons were tough all-around, as Palffy struggled to get accustomed to a new country, a new culture, and a new language.

To grasp English, Palffy devoured bad TV sit-coms and B-grade American movies. The plots were simple. Slowly, he became more at ease with the language. As he did, he became more confident on and off the ice. The 1995–96 season would be Palffy's breakthrough year, when he scored 43 goals and 44 assists for 87 points. He showed it was no fluke the following year, scoring 48 goals and 42 assists for 90 points.

The Islanders had a scoring sensation it could build a top line around. "Just this year [1997–98] he's become real comfortable with the atmosphere in Long Island and knowing his role," said teammate Scott Lachance. "He jokes around a lot more than he used to and shows us all sides. He loosened up last year, but it's now more recognizable."

"It's easier to communicate with my teammates," says Palffy. "I'm having more fun now than two, three years ago." The addition of Czech Robert Reichel also helped. Reichel became more than a linemate and roomie on the road. He became a soulmate for Palffy, one who literally spoke the same language.

When Palffy is on, he seems almost to dance on

the ice. He has deceptive quickness and is an elusive skater with a lightning first step, the hallmark of similar-sized stars such as Paul Kariya, Pavel Bure, and Peter Bondra.

"He won't burn around people, but when there's an opening he can get to it in a hurry," says the *Hockey Scouting Report*. "When you are a player of Palffy's size and surrounded on the NHL scoring list by the likes of Jaromir Jagr and Brendan Shanahan, you are doing something right. Palffy has excellent hands for passing or shooting."

Like many of the best small players in the league, Palffy has found a way to survive in a jungle of behemoths several inches taller and many, many pounds heavier. He never puts himself in a position to get bowled over by an opponent.

"He's not really a soft player but he won't go into the corner if he's going to get crunched," says the *Scouting Report*. "But he wants the puck."

This season, Palffy led his team again with 45 goals and 42 assists for 87 points. However, he could only view the season as a disappointment because his team missed the playoffs again. Former Islander coach Rick Bowness says there is a 60-goal season waiting to burst out of the player soon.

"There will be a point in Ziggy's career where he will score 60 goals," said Bowness. "That's probably not even a challenge. He can do that. That's how good he is. He's one of the more prolific goal scor-

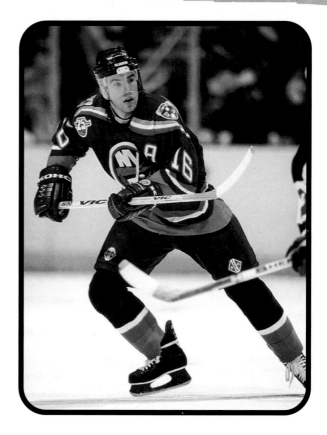

ers in this league today. He's one of the most exciting players to watch in this league today.

"And he's going to get better."

Today, Palffy sits on the doorstep of NHL superstardom. He'd like his whole team to take the next step with him.

"If it's going to happen, it's going to happen," Palffy said. "It would be nice for the team and for me, but if it's going to happen it's going to be with a lot of help from the guys."

(#16) ZIGMUND PALFFY, New York Islanders, right wing

| YEAR | TEAM | LEA | REGULAR SEASON | | | | | PLAYOFFS | | | | |
			GP	G	A	TP	PIM	GP	G	A	TP	PIM
1990-91	Nitra	Czech.	50	34	16	50	18	.....	.....	.....	.....	.....
1991-92	Dukla Trencin	Czech.	45	41	33	74	36	.....	.....	.....	.....	.....
1992-93	Dukla Trencin	Czech.	43	38	41	79	.....	.....	.....	.....	.....	.....
1993-94	NY Islanders	NHL	5	0	0	0	0	.....	.....	.....	.....	.....
	Salt Lake	IHL	57	25	32	57	83	.....	.....	.....	.....	.....
1994-95	Denver	IHL	33	20	23	43	40	.....	.....	.....	.....	.....
	NY Islanders	NHL	33	10	7	17	6	.....	.....	.....	.....	.....
1995-96	NY Islanders	NHL	81	43	44	87	56	.....	.....	.....	.....	.....
1996-97	Dukla Trencin	Slovak	1	0	0	0	.....	.....	.....	.....	.....	.....
	NY Islanders	NHL	80	48	42	90	43	.....	.....	.....	.....	.....
1997-98	NY Islanders	NHL	82	45	42	87	34	.....	.....	.....	.....	.....

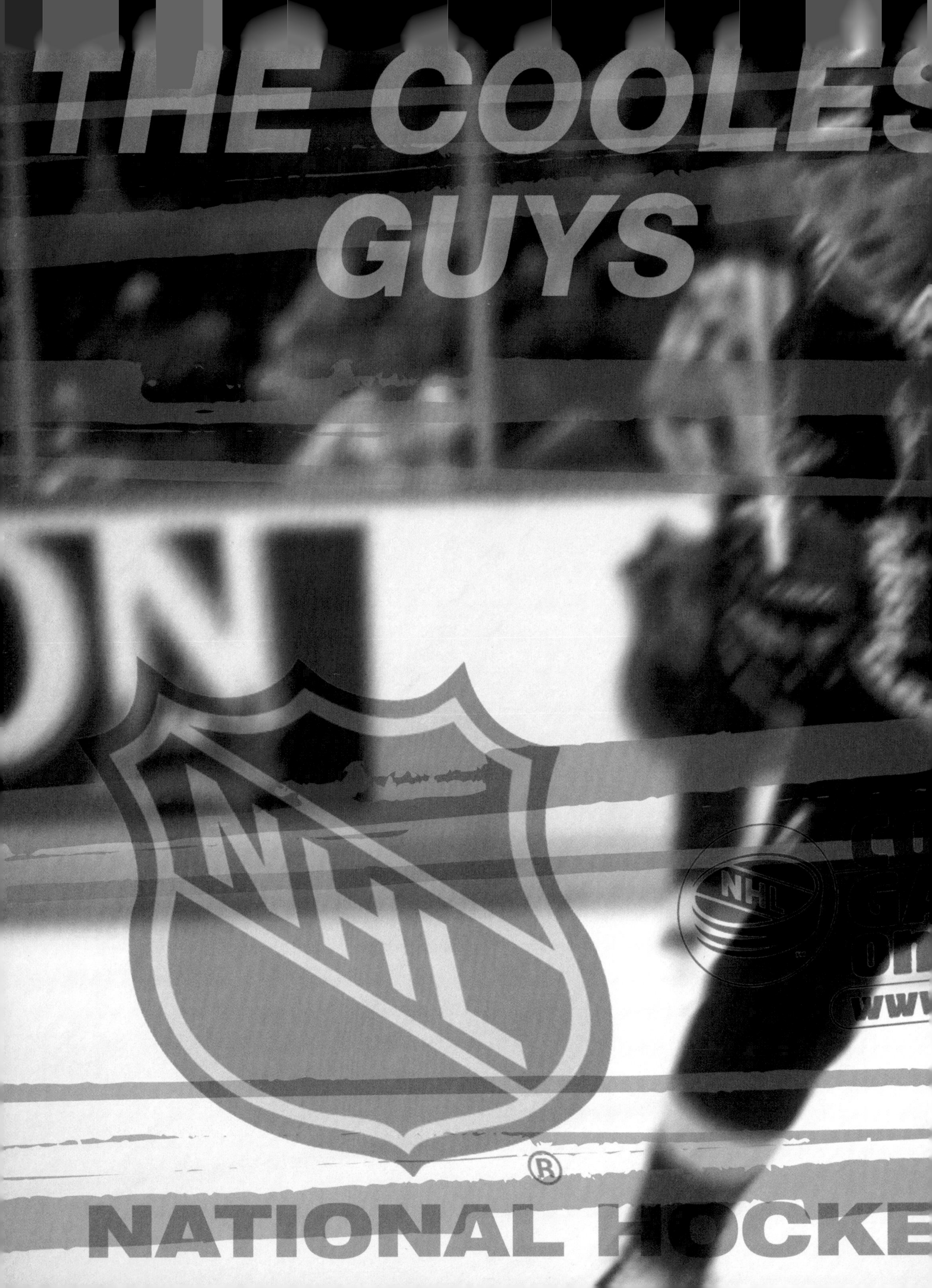
THE COOLES
GUYS
NHL
NATIONAL HOCKE

Power Forwards

Going Through Defenders

To Go To The Net

Tony Amonte

Chicago Blackhawks

It started out as a gimmick. Chicago Blackhawks forward Tony Amonte thought he'd let his hair grow for fun. But when his offensive numbers began growing along with his mane, he decided he'd keep his flowing locks. Regardless of what his mom thought.

"She would call and ask me when I was going to stop looking like a bum," Amonte remembers of his first season with long hair. "I hated it," says his mom, Kathy. "I thought he was too handsome to have hair like that. I know he's superstitious but it

was getting ridiculous." And as the American-born Amonte became an NHL scoring star, the hair became a perfect target for fans in opposition rinks.

"The fans would yell at me: 'Get a haircut!' And the more they yelled, the longer I wanted to grow it. It was fun. I'm also a little superstitious and I kept scoring. So I figured, 'Why bother cutting it?'"

> ## "He has fun doing everything, especially playing."
> ### —Lewis Amonte

His sister's wedding this past year forced Amonte to break down finally and get his hair chopped. When he began this past season with his new look he discovered an amazing thing: he could still put the puck in the net. It wasn't just the long hair after all. His flowing mane did, however, seem perfectly suited to Amonte's dashing style of play. Today, he remains one of the most exciting forwards in the game.

A game that was in his blood early. "Tony started so young and got so good so fast," says his father, Lewis. "I remember sitting in the den when he was four or five and watching him walk around—but he

wasn't walking, he was skating across the carpet in his socks. Swoosh, swoosh, swoosh. It's all he ever wanted. Tony became an intense player who wanted to win, but he was easy-going, too. He has fun doing everything, especially playing."

Amonte, 27, is from the Boston suburb of Hingham and played his high school hockey at elite Thayer Academy. His linemate at Thayer was Jeremy Roenick. The pair helped Thayer win two New England high school championships, the first one over a team led by future NHL Superstar, Brian Leetch. Amonte and Roenick were magic together—an act that would be repeated later in the NHL.

Amonte was the youngest player selected in the 1988 NHL Entry Draft, picked in the third round—68th overall—by the New York Rangers. He was still in high school then, still playing with Roenick. While Roenick would go from high school to the NHL, Amonte played two seasons at Boston University before signing with New York on April 2, 1991.

In his first two professional seasons, Amonte played alongside Ranger captain Mark Messier and right winger Adam Graves. He scored 35 goals as a rookie, getting the nod from the *Hockey News* and the *Sporting News* as rookie of the year. However, he finished second along with Nicklas Lidstrom as runner up to Pavel Bure for the Calder Trophy. Amonte continued to shine in his sophomore season, bagging 33 goals and adding 43 assists for 76 points. However, when Mike Keenan arrived the following season to take over behind the Ranger bench, Amonte discovered his style of play wasn't to the new coach's liking. Keenan favored a more physical type of player and soon Amonte was off to Chicago where he would be reunited with Roenick.

The two formed the nucleus of the Hawks' top line, helping the team reach the conference finals in 1994–95. The following year the Hawks had a thrilling second-round series against Colorado but fell short against the eventual Stanley Cup winners that year.

That season would mark the end of the short-lived reunion of Amonte and Roenick, who was traded to the Phoenix Coyotes. "I loved playing with J.R. It was a dream of ours to play on the same club in the NHL," said Amonte. "Coming up through the ranks, J.R. was always the premier player. I just tried to keep up with him. Our time together in Chicago was great."

While he missed his good friend, J.R., the trade thrust Amonte into his team's offensive spotlight. He would shine, and 1996–97 would be a season like no other. Before the NHL campaign began, Amonte played a starring role in the upset victory by the U.S. over Canada in the World Cup. He scored the championship-winning goal in the final game in Montreal. Amonte followed it with a career-best 41 goals, during a season that would be highlighted by his first NHL All-Star Game appearance. His play would be rewarded, as Amonte signed a five-year contract that would keep him in the Windy City through the millennium.

"It was like a dream," said Amonte of his dream season. "Things just seemed to be going my way. The World Cup might have been the greatest thrill I've ever had in hockey, and it gave me a boost going into the season. I came back with a lot of confidence, really believing in myself. Then the goals kept coming."

Former teammate and Blackhawks star Denis Savard recognized a change in Amonte's game. "His game has gone to the next level. When he gets the chance to score, he's going to get there." His buddy and former linemate, J.R., also recognized his friend's emerging greatness.

"Tony is a dynamic player and deserves all the credit in the world," said Roenick. "He's one of the best guys in the game, in my opinion." This past season, Amonte continued to shine through an otherwise overcast year for a Blackhawks team that failed to make the playoffs. Amonte led the Hawks with 31 goals and 42 assists.

Tony Amonte remains at the top of his game.

"He will enjoy this part of his life," says Savard. "He is going to want to score every night and I know how he thinks. I know he thinks every day, 'God, I can't wait to score tonight.'"

#10 TONY AMONTE, Chicago Blackhawks, right wing

| YEAR | TEAM | LEA | REGULAR SEASON | | | | | PLAYOFFS | | | | |
			GP	G	A	TP	PIM	GP	G	A	TP	PIM
1989-90	Boston U.	H.E.	41	25	33	58	52	.....	.....	.....	.....	.....
1990-91	Boston U.	H.E.	38	31	37	68	82	.....	.....	.....	.....	.....
	NY Rangers	NHL	.....	.....	.....	.....	.....	2	0	2	2	2
1991-92	NY Rangers	NHL	79	35	34	69	55	13	3	6	9	2
1992-93	NY Rangers	NHL	83	33	43	76	49	.....	.....	.....	.....	.....
1993-94	NY Rangers	NHL	72	16	22	38	31	.....	.....	.....	.....	.....
	Chicago	NHL	7	1	3	4	6	6	4	2	6	4
1994-95	Fassa	Italy	14	22	16	38	10	.....	.....	.....	.....	.....
	Chicago	NHL	48	15	20	35	41	16	3	3	6	10
1995-96	Chicago	NHL	81	31	32	63	62	7	2	4	6	6
1996-97	Chicago	NHL	81	41	36	77	64	6	4	2	6	8
1997-98	Chicago	NHL	82	31	42	73	66	.....	.....	.....	.....	.....

John LeClair

Back in the early '90s, when John LeClair was with the Montreal Canadiens, he had a pair of seasons in which he scored 19 goals.

Not bad, thought the left winger, I've probably reached my potential.

At the time, recalls LeClair, he thought of himself as "a third-line checking forward who could go up and down the wing, not hurt the team and maybe chip in with a goal once in a while."

Once in a while ended up being pretty darned often.

"I want to be respected around the league, but it's not my goal to be the top left wing. What matters to me is what matters to the guys in the dressing room."

In each of his last three seasons as a Philadelphia Flyer, LeClair has hit, or bettered, the 50-goal mark. In 1997–98, he was his team's top point man, scoring 51 goals and adding 36 assists for 87 points. In each of the previous two years, he accumulated a staggering 97 points.

You'd think the guy's head would have become a tad swollen by now. But that's not John LeClair.

"I want to be respected around the league, but it's not my goal to be the top left wing," he says.

"What matters to me is what matters to the guys in the dressing room."

Modest, and considerate, too. That's not something you can say about every professional athlete. But then, there's nothing that's particularly typical about John LeClair.

He was, for instance, the first U.S.-born player ever picked by the Montreal Canadiens—that was back in the 1987 NHL Entry Draft. He was the first player in the Stanley Cup's illustrious history to score back-to-back overtime winners in the 1993 series final against Los Angeles. And yes, he was the first guy to take the Stanley Cup to Camp Ta-Kum-Ta, a summer getaway for children with cancer, not far from his home in St. Albans, Vermont.

That, says LeClair's childhood buddy, Mark Toof, was absolutely typical of his friend, someone "with a huge heart [who] never forgets where he comes from."

It was in a modest home in St. Albans that LeClair grew up, playing hockey in the winters and soccer and baseball the rest of the year.

After years on the ice—both in organized youth leagues and out on the backyard rink—LeClair starred at Bellows Free Academy. His reputation began to develop, and coaches from everywhere began to show up and take a look.

"From the time we had the first person call us until after he committed to UVM [the University of Vermont] there was not a single evening that he didn't get a call from someone, sometimes several calls," says LeClair's mother, Bev. In the spring of LeClair's senior year at Bellows, another phone call came. It was the night of the NHL Entry Draft.

"The telephone rang and there was a French-speaking lady on the line," recalls Butch LeClair, John's dad. "I knew right away who had drafted him."

A week after his final game with the University of Vermont, LeClair made his debut with the Canadiens in the Montreal Forum—and scored a goal. It would be the first of many in the NHL.

LeClair says there's no debating what qualifies as

his best hockey memory. That would have happened in 1993, when Montreal clinched its 24th Stanley Cup.

Two years later, Philadelphia made a successful bid for the solid, 6' 3", 226-pound left winger. It took no time for the club to realize the prize it had acquired. LeClair quickly began setting career highs for goals and assists and became known as a member of the Flyers' infamous Legion of Doom, a powerhouse line that included center Eric Lindros and right wing Mikael Renberg.

Still, LeClair hung on to his humility.

"Never in my wildest dreams did I think I'd become a 50-goal scorer," he says. "If you look back on it, it's not like I played great hockey every single night. A lot of those 50 goals have to be attributed to my teammates."

As LeClair's momentum grew, so did support for the John LeClair Foundation, an organization set up by LeClair and his friends to benefit needy children and youth groups in Vermont. The foundation initially set a modest goal of $5,000, but in its first four years it distributed more than $100,000 to numerous groups, including Camp Ta-Kum-Ta.

The 29-year-old LeClair, who was named 1997 winner of the Humanitarian of the Year Award as presented by the Philadelphia chapter of the Professional Sports Writers Association, is as committed to people as he is to his game.

"I just think it's a satisfying opportunity to show appreciation for the support of the whole state," says LeClair. "Through the foundation, I can give something back."

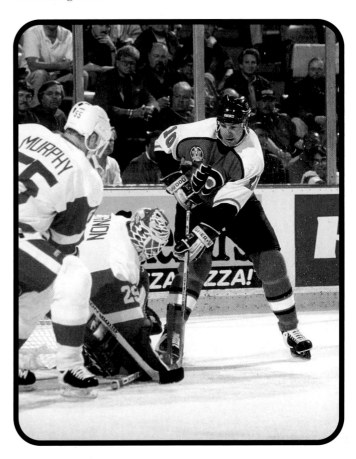

#10 JOHN LECLAIR, Philadelphia Flyers, left wing

YEAR	TEAM	LEA	REGULAR SEASON					PLAYOFFS				
			GP	G	A	TP	PIM	GP	G	A	TP	PIM
1987-88	U. of Vermont	ECAC	31	12	22	34	62	.....	.....	.....	.....	.....
1988-89	U. of Vermont	ECAC	18	9	12	21	40	.....	.....	.....	.....	.....
1989-90	U. of Vermont	ECAC	10	10	6	16	38	.....	.....	.....	.....	.....
1990-91	U. of Vermont	ECAC	33	25	20	45	58	.....	.....	.....	.....	.....
	Montreal	NHL	10	2	5	7	2	3	0	0	0	0
1991-92	Montreal	NHL	59	8	11	19	14	8	1	1	2	4
	Fredericton	AHL	8	7	7	14	10	2	0	0	0	4
1992-93	Montreal	NHL	72	19	25	44	33	20	4	6	10	14
1993-94	Montreal	NHL	74	19	24	43	32	7	2	1	3	8
1994-95	Montreal	NHL	9	1	4	5	10	.....	.....	.....	.....	.....
	Philadelphia	NHL	37	25	24	49	20	15	5	7	12	4
1995-96	Philadelphia	NHL	82	51	46	97	64	11	6	5	11	6
1996-97	Philadelphia	NHL	82	50	47	97	58	19	9	12	21	10
1997-98	Philadelphia	NHL	82	51	36	87	32	5	1	1	2	8

Mark Recchi

Montreal Canadiens

They call him the Iron Man. They call him the Wrecking Ball.

A coach once called him a pit bull.

It doesn't matter which label you prefer—they all amount to the same thing. Mark Recchi, star of the Montreal Canadiens, is one tough hockey player.

"Game in, game out, he's been the team's hardest worker, its soul each night, and not just to put numbers on the board," observes Montreal sports writer Red Fisher. "He always brings a physical game to the arena—a special measure of give-and-take only a few of the NHL's untouchables can deliver."

In the 1997–98 season, Recchi was by far the top point man for the Canadiens, scoring 32 goals and adding 42 assists for 74 points. A year earlier, the numbers were 34 and 46, for 80.

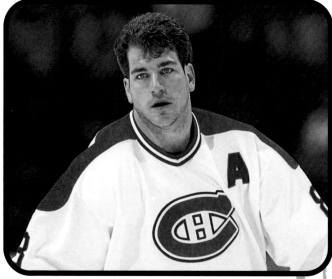

Pretty astounding, especially considering that Recchi was at one time thought to be too small to play in the big leagues. The right winger, who hails from Kamloops, British Columbia, stands 5' 10" and weighs 185 pounds. He went undrafted in his first two years of eligibility, and was eventually picked—by Pittsburgh, in 1988—in the fourth round of his third draft year.

> ## He has, they say, the resiliency of a rubber band: you can knock him down but he'll bounce right back.

When he finally did make it, his father couldn't contain his joy.

"It's a feeling that I really can't describe," Mel Recchi said after seeing Mark playing with Pittsburgh in the Stanley Cup Finals. "It's like a dream, all those years watching the finals on TV with [Bryan] Trottier and [Guy] Lafleur and now I'm watching my son."

Recchi's best season with Pittsburgh came in 1990–91, the year the Penguins took the Cup. He scored 40 goals that year and assisted on 73 others for a point total of 113.

In 1992 Recchi was part of a huge seven-player, three-team swap that saw him go the Philadelphia Flyers. He stayed in the City of Brotherly Love until 1995 when the Canadiens picked him up.

Recchi—the guy one-time Canadiens' coach Mario Tremblay called a pit bull—has not been a disappointment.

He has, they say, the resiliency of a rubber band: you can knock him down but he'll bounce right back. You can shove him into the boards, but he'll spring immediately back into action.

"Recchi is a little package with a lot of firepower," says the *Hockey Scouting Report*. "He is one of the top small players in the game, and certainly one of the most productive."

Productive, and also reliable. In the 1997–98 regular season, he played in more games than any other Canadien—all 82 of them. At the end of the previous season, he had played in 472 consecutive games, including playoffs, and had not missed a game since March 31, 1991.

That's some employment record.

The Iron Man has a reputation for grit, for feistiness, for perseverance. He also has a dangerous shot.

"Although he is not as dynamic as Maurice Richard, he likes to use the Richard cut-back while rifling a wrist shot back across," says the *Report*. "He resembles a puck magnet because he is always going where the puck is."

Kevin Constantine, coach of the Pittsburgh Penguins, observes that the 30-year-old Recchi pretty much has it all.

"He's fast, he's got a great shot and he's got a history of scoring goals," he says.

Montreal winger Shayne Corson agrees.

"Before I played with him, I thought he was more or less just an offensive player. But he's altered his game. He's more physical, too. He can hit all night long."

Yes, he can—no matter what team he's on. Recchi has made NHL All-Star Game appearances and has represented Team Canada in three World Championships, including the 1997 round in which Canada took gold. He also traveled to Nagano,

Japan, in early 1998 to represent his country in the Winter Olympics.

Recchi, dogged fighter, has had the last laugh on the clubs that overlooked him way back when. He was never huge, but that's turned out to be inconsequential. Mark Recchi is still a warrior made of iron.

#8 MARK RECCHI, Montreal Canadiens, right wing

YEAR	TEAM	LEA	REGULAR SEASON					PLAYOFFS				
			GP	G	A	TP	PIM	GP	G	A	TP	PIM
1985-86	N. Westminster	WHL	72	21	40	61	55	.....	.....	.....	.....	.....
1986-87	Kamloops	WHL	40	26	50	76	63	13	3	16	19	17
1987-88	Kamloops	WHL	62	61	93	154	75	17	10	21	31	18
1988-89	Pittsburgh	NHL	15	1	1	2	0	.....	.....	.....	.....	.....
	Muskegon	IHL	63	50	49	99	86	14	7	14	21	28
1989-90	Pittsburgh	NHL	74	30	37	67	44	.....	.....	.....	.....	.....
	Muskegon	IHL	4	7	4	11	2	.....	.....	.....	.....	.....
1990-91	Pittsburgh	NHL	78	40	73	113	48	24	10	24	34	33
1991-92	Pittsburgh	NHL	58	33	37	70	78	.....	.....	.....	.....	.....
	Philadelphia	NHL	22	10	17	27	18	.....	.....	.....	.....	.....
1992-93	Philadelphia	NHL	84	53	70	123	95	.....	.....	.....	.....	.....
1993-94	Philadelphia	NHL	84	40	67	107	46	.....	.....	.....	.....	.....
1994-95	Philadelphia	NHL	10	2	3	5	12	.....	.....	.....	.....	.....
	Montreal	NHL	39	14	29	43	16	.....	.....	.....	.....	.....
1995-96	Montreal	NHL	82	28	50	78	69	6	3	3	6	0
1996-97	Montreal	NHL	82	34	46	80	58	5	4	2	6	2
1997-98	Montreal	NHL	82	32	42	74	51	10	4	8	12	6

Brendan Shanahan

Detroit Red Wings

Never believe what you read—especially when it applies to Brendan Shanahan. True to his Irish roots, the Detroit left-winger has been known to spin a tale or two. He's said he was once a cattle rancher and a professional soccer goalie. He's claimed to have been an extra in the movie *Forrest Gump*, to have run with the bulls in Pamplona, to have spent his summers in an Irish manor.

He's said he played the saxophone, but was snagged on that little fib the day a television crew from St. Louis showed up at a practice with a rented saxophone. "Sorry," he's reported to have told them. "No sax on game days." If all this illustrates anything, it's that Shanahan loves a good story. The 29-year-old Mimico, Ontario, native may not have

finished high school, but that didn't prevent him from becoming educated. He adores F. Scott Fitzgerald and J.R.R. Tolkein and Leon Uris. He reads Tennyson and can recite Shakespeare.

"Shanny shoots so hard it can go right through you." — Chris Osgood

"He's always loved stories," says Brian Shanahan, one of Brendan's three older brothers. "If I read a book, he'd want me to tell him the whole thing. He was seven or eight and I'd just finished [Ken Follett's] *Eye of the Needle* and he made me tell him every detail. He'd ask 'Did you skip a part?'"

Clearly, this is a multidimensional man, a guy who loves hockey, but still makes time to surf the Internet. This is a man with personality, a 220-pound, 6' 3" passionate Irishman who would, says *Sports Illustrated*, "look a little like Liam Neeson if Liam Neeson were really handsome."

Oh, and yes, he's not too bad on the ice. This past season, he knocked in 28 goals for the Red Wings—nine of them game-winners—and added 29 assists. Last year, when the Wings took the Stanley Cup, he finished first in overall team scoring, with 47 goals and 41 assists.

It's been over a decade now since Shanahan first entered the NHL. It was back in the 1987 Entry Draft that Shanahan, who'd played junior hockey with the Ontario Hockey League, went to New Jersey as first pick. In 1991 he signed as a free agent with St. Louis, and was traded to Hartford four years later. Last year, he was a key component in Detroit's first Stanley Cup victory since 1955, scoring three goals and collecting an assist in the final series against Philadelphia.

Observers agree that if there's one thing that distinguishes Shanahan's game, one thing that places it a cut above, it's his punishing one-timer.

"It is a great weapon," says Red Wing teammate, center Igor Larionov. "He has one of the best one-timers in the league, he and Brett Hull.

"There are no bad passes to Shanny. Any pass you make to him is OK because he can find a way to handle the puck and put it in with a one-timer or a second touch. If I have two guys available for a shot, I prefer Shanny to take it because he has an accurate shot and his release is just incredible."

No one knows the power of Shanahan's shots better than Red Wing goalie Chris Osgood.

"Shanny shoots so hard it can go right through you," says Osgood. "In practice, he usually lays off his shot because he doesn't want to hurt us. But sometimes, if he hasn't scored in a few games, he gets in a bad mood and lets 'em rip."

Shanahan would have given anything, of course, to have seen Canada bring home a medal from the Winter Olympics in Nagano, but that was not to be. Had he returned with a medal, there's little doubt he would have dedicated it to his father, Donal, an immigrant from County Cork, who used to take his four sons to Toronto's rinks in the early dawn, then sit back, smoke his pipe, and read his newspaper.

Donal died of Alzheimer's Disease before Brendan made it to the NHL. Ever since, when Shanahan stands on the ice listening to the national anthem being played, he looks upward and thinks of his father. Even in Nagano, Shanahan said, his dad was on his mind.

Clearly, Shanahan is as deep as he is gregarious, as thoughtful as he is charming. He's a hockey player who feels the highs and lows, and who's driven by a range of emotions.

"I'm definitely an emotional player," he says. "I

play better when I'm emotional. But to play with that emotion you have to fight some battles, experience life in the trenches—some wins and losses—before you get to that special feeling of wanting to play for the logo on the front of the sweater and the other guys who are wearing it."

#14 BRENDAN SHANAHAN, Detroit Red Wings, left wing

YEAR	TEAM	LEA	REGULAR SEASON					PLAYOFFS				
			GP	G	A	TP	PIM	GP	G	A	TP	PIM
1985-86	London	OHL	59	28	34	62	70	5	5	5	10	5
1986-87	London	OHL	56	39	53	92	92	.....	.....	.....	.....	.....
1987-88	New Jersey	NHL	65	7	19	26	131	12	2	1	3	44
1988-89	New Jersey	NHL	68	22	28	50	115	.....	.....	.....	.....	.....
1989-90	New Jersey	NHL	73	30	42	72	137	6	3	3	6	20
1990-91	New Jersey	NHL	75	29	37	66	141	7	3	5	8	12
1991-92	St. Louis	NHL	80	33	36	69	171	6	2	3	5	14
1992-93	St. Louis	NHL	71	51	43	94	174	11	4	3	7	18
1993-94	St. Louis	NHL	81	52	50	102	211	4	2	5	7	4
	Dusseldorf	Ger.	3	5	3	8	4	.....	.....	.....	.....	.....
	St. Louis	NHL	45	20	21	41	136	5	4	5	9	14
1995-96	Hartford	NHL	74	44	34	78	125	.....	.....	.....	.....	.....
1996-97	Hartford	NHL	2	1	0	1	0	.....	.....	.....	.....	.....
	Detroit	NHL	79	46	41	87	131	20	9	8	17	43
1997-98	Detroit	NHL	75	28	29	57	154	20	5	4	9	22

Keith Tkachuk

Phoenix Coyotes

He's the face of American hockey in the 1990s. Tough as steel, as nasty as they come. Phoenix Coyotes forward Keith Tkachuk is one of the most intimidating players in the National Hockey League.

He's The Terminator with a scoring touch.

"Definite mean streak," says Mike Smith, who was general manager of the Winnipeg Jets, the team with whom Tkachuk broke into the NHL.

"Keith likes to hurt people," says former teammate Dean Kennedy. "Tkachuk is volatile and mean as a scorpion," says the *Hockey Scouting Report*. You get the idea. Tkachuk will never skate around an opponent when skating through him is an option. He's a player who will tell you his best night at the rink is when he gets a Gordie Howe hat trick—a goal, an assist, and a fight.

At 26, Keith Tkachuk is simply one of the best players in the game—period. And he's just entering his prime.

"I've been hit by everybody," says Dallas Stars forward Brett Hull, a teammate of Tkachuk on recent U.S. Olympic and World Cup hockey squads. "No question about it, he's tough. He's the guy everybody wants on their team. There aren't many players, if any, that can score that many goals and penalty minutes. I mean, those kind of players are few and far between."

He's The Terminator with a scoring touch.

In 1997–98, Tkachuk's numbers were down slightly in all categories from the stellar year he enjoyed the season before. But they were impressive nonetheless. This past season, he scored 40 goals and added 26 assists—to lead his team. He also had 147 penalty minutes. In 1996–97, Tkachuk's best in the NHL, he scored a league-leading 52 goals and had 34 assists for 86 points. He also racked up 228 penalty minutes. Tkachuk has one of the highest IQs in hockey—as in Intimidation Quotient.

The *Hockey News* established the IQ award to recognize a player's talent (at least 30 goals) and toughness (at least 100 penalty minutes, not including misconducts). Tkachuk has won the award three times in the six seasons it's been awarded.

The son of a fire chief, Tkachuk was born in east Boston, in a tough, working-class neighborhood known as Jeffrey's Point. Mother, Geraldine, ran the house and kept watch over Keith, his brother, and two sisters. The Tkachuks never had piles of money but always had fun. "We were always outside, playing street hockey, baseball, football, startin' fights, you name it," Tkachuk says.

About 100 yards from the Tkachuk home was an outdoor rink. The Tkachuk boys would own it. And young Keith would develop a feisty, aggressive style of play early on. In his freshman year at Malden Catholic High School, Keith made the varsity team. By 1990, he was considered the top high school prospect in the country.

"He was overpowering," recalls Mark Tarmey, Keith's high school coach. "He was a hard-nosed, tough city kid. There may have been other players with as much talent, but I'll say this: Keith's work habits are why he's in the NHL."

Not surprisingly, Tkachuk was a big Boston Bruins fan. And his favorite player? Cam Neely, of course. His favorite movie of all time remains *Slap Shot*, the cult hockey film about three brothers who fight their way through a semiprofessional hockey league.

In his senior year of high school, Tkachuk was drafted in the first round by the Winnipeg Jets. However, he opted to play one year at Boston University where he played alongside future NHL stars Tony Amonte and Shawn McEachern. In 1992–93, Tkachuk's first full season with the Jets, he established his reputation for a smash-mouth style of play, rolling up 201 penalty minutes along the way.

At the start of his second season, the Jets caught the attention of the hockey world when they named Tkachuk their captain—the youngest player on the team and youngest captain in the league. The message was clear: this was someone special.

At the start of the 1995–96 season, the Chicago Blackhawks made Tkachuk a $17-million contract offer. Winnipeg had a choice—match the offer or lose the player. It came at a time when the franchise was struggling financially, and Tkachuk became a symbol in the Canadian city of greedy, multimillionaire athletes who were driving the game out of small-market towns like theirs. The Jets had no choice and matched the offer.

The Jets would relocate to Phoenix for the start of the 1996–97 season, marking a new chapter in Tkachuk's career. He would end up playing with Jeremy Roenick, a fellow Bostonian who had a style similiar to his own—a Big Bad Bruins style.

In 1996, Tkachuk was an integral part of the U.S. World Cup hockey team that beat Canada. More than anyone, Tkachuk served notice the U.S. was an emerging hockey superpower and would no longer play second fiddle to anyone.

Mike Gartner, an NHL veteran and teammate of Tkachuk's on the Coyotes, says the Phoenix captain is a unique player. "So much of it is just plain natural, stuff you can't teach or learn. When I think of Keith, I think of him as a complete player. There are no weaknesses in his game. But he's constantly striving to make himself better."

More than anything else, Tkachuk says, he wants to be known as a winner. "I'm moving up

into my prime," he says. "As captain of this team, it's up to me to lead this team to the Stanley Cup. That's my goal and this is the team I want to celebrate with."

And he's not going to let anyone stand in his way.

#7 KEITH TKACHUK, Phoenix Coyotes, left wing

			REGULAR SEASON					PLAYOFFS				
YEAR	TEAM	LEA	GP	G	A	TP	PIM	GP	G	A	TP	PIM
1990-91	Boston U.	H.E.	36	17	23	40	70	.....	.....	.....	.....	.....
1991-92	U.S. National		45	10	10	20	141	.....	.....	.....	.....	.....
	US Olympic		8	1	1	2	12	.....	.....	.....	.....	.....
	Winnipeg	NHL	17	3	5	8	28	7	3	0	3	30
1992-93	Winnipeg	NHL	83	28	23	51	201	6	4	0	4	14
1993-94	Winnipeg	NHL	84	41	40	81	255	.....	.....	.....	.....	.....
1994-95	Winnipeg	NHL	48	22	29	51	152	.....	.....	.....	.....	.....
1995-96	Winnipeg	NHL	76	50	48	98	156	6	1	2	3	22
1996-97	Phoenix	NHL	81	52	34	86	228	7	6	0	6	7
1997-98	Phoenix	NHL	69	40	26	66	147	6	3	3	6	10

End2End

Offensive Defensemen

Who Lead the Rush

Roman Hamrlik

Edmonton Oilers

Like many kids growing up, Roman Hamrlik had a backup plan in case his dreams to be a professional hockey player didn't pan out. He was going to be a cook.

Growing up in Zlin, in the Czech Republic, Hamrlik decided cooking would be an easier life than working in the local tire plant where his father slogged away 12 hours a day.

But pucks, not omelettes, were always young Roman's first choice, and his skill on skates was advanced early enough that he was awarded entry in the prestigious Zlin School for Athletes.

Soon all the young hockey player could think of was following in the footsteps of countrymen such as Petr Klima and Jaromir Jagr, who both left the

Czech Republic to pursue fame and riches in the National Hockey League. "As kids we used to read all about those guys and the NHL," said Hamrlik. "People like Petr and them, they were heroes to us. That's what I wanted. I wanted to play in the NHL like they were. More than anything."

> "You get a guy who can shoot like he can and there's a buzz in the crowd. He gets the shots on the net."
> — Curtis Joseph

It didn't take long for NHL scouts to hear about the amazing talents of a certain young Czech defenseman.

"There was nothing else out there like him," said John Chapman, the former Tampa Bay Lightning scout who played a major role in the team's decision to draft Hamrlik first overall in 1992.

"He was the complete package."

The jump to the NHL is never easy. There is always a period of transition. However, it can some-times be tougher for someone from a foreign country, who has to adjust not only to a superior brand of hockey but also to a different language and culture.

"The language was the toughest part," said Hamrlik. "There was no one to really talk to. Except for family. But sometimes you want to talk to other people and you can't. It was hard."

Hamrlik wears a different uniform today. Now, he's an Edmonton Oiler. A uniform that Edmonton Oilers GM Glen Sather hopes will bring out the best in the promising young defenseman.

"You might go 5, 10 years in this league running a hockey team and never have the opportunity to get a player like this," said Sather. "He can be a world-class player."

Former Oilers goaltender Curtis Joseph, now with the Toronto Maple Leafs, was happy he would no longer have to face Hamrlik's titanic blasts from the blueline.

"I'd say he's got one of the five hardest shots from the point in the league," said Joseph.

"You get a guy who can shoot like he can and there's a buzz in the crowd. He gets the shots on the net."

Veteran Oilers defenseman Kevin Lowe, who won

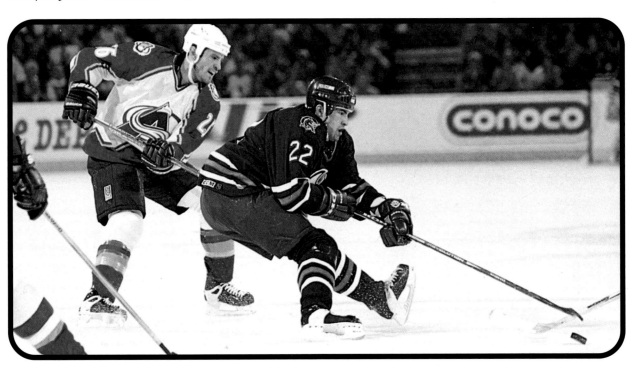

his first Stanley Cup when the 24-year-old Hamrlik was still in elementary school, says Hamrlik is developed beyond his years.

"When we played him in New York he was one of those guys that we targeted," said Lowe, remembering his days in a Ranger uniform. "We wanted to wear him down, like Ray Bourque."

Which would be the highest compliment you could pay Hamrlik, who counts the All-Star Boston Bruins defenseman as one of his heroes. In the 1996 NHL All-Star Game in Boston, Hamrlik was paired with Bourque.

"It was a great thrill," said Hamrlik. "Bourque is still the best in the league." Wayne Cashman, formerly with the Lightning and now an assistant coach in Philadelphia, sees a comparison between Hamrlik and Bourque. "He's doing the kinds of things that a Bourque does now," said Cashman. "The way he controls the game and works at both ends of the ice. There are only a few guys in the league who can do that."

Hamrlik, according to the *Hockey Scouting Report*, has all the tools to become the NHL's next star defenseman.

"He is a fast, strong skater forwards and backwards," says the *Report* of the 6'2", 200-pound blueliner. "He is a mobile defenseman with a solid shot and good passing skills, though he is very creative."

Hamrlik finished the 1997–98 season with 9 goals and 32 assists, good for 41 points and fifth

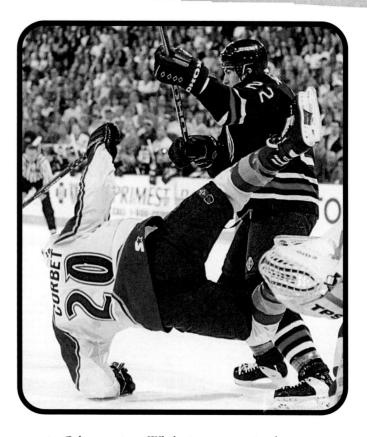

spot in Oiler scoring. While it was a point better than his numbers the previous season, it was off from his career high of 65 points in 1995–96.

Edmonton's high-flying, offensive-minded system seems a perfect fit for Hamrlik. It helps that the Oiler dressing room resonates with a rich history that Hamrlik was aware of growing up in another part of the world. "When I lived back home I always tried to get information about their great players like Wayne Gretzky and Mark Messier," remembers Hamrlik. "It was always my dream and now I am here."

#22 ROMAN HAMRLIK, Edmonton Oilers, defense

| YEAR | TEAM | LEA | REGULAR SEASON | | | | | PLAYOFFS | | | | |
			GP	G	A	TP	PIM	GP	G	A	TP	PIM
1990-91	TJ Zlin	Czech	14	2	2	4	18	.....	.....	.....	.....	.....
1991-92	ZPS Zin	Czech	34	5	5	10	50	.....	.....	.....	.....	.....
1992-93	Tampa Bay	NHL	67	6	15	21	71	.....	.....	.....	.....	.....
	Atlanta	IHL	2	1	1	2	2	.....	.....	.....	.....	.....
1993-94	Tampa Bay	NHL	64	3	18	21	135	.....	.....	.....	.....	.....
1994-95	ZPS Zin	Czech.	2	1	0	1	10	.....	.....	.....	.....	.....
	Tampa Bay	NHL	48	12	11	23	86	.....	.....	.....	.....	.....
1995-96	Tampa Bay	NHL	82	16	49	65	103	5	0	1	1	4
1996-97	Tampa Bay	NHL	79	12	28	40	57	.....	.....	.....	.....	.....
1997-98	Tampa Bay	NHL	37	3	12	15	22					
	Edmonton	NHL	41	6	20	26	48	12	0	6	6	12

Brian Leetch

New York Rangers

He is, say those who know him, one of the most quiet, most unassuming guys around. The kind who prefers not to initiate conversation, but to speak when spoken to. The kind who has a habit of showering after a game, then dressing and slipping away unnoticed.

Brian Leetch is not what you'd call a publicity seeker.

"I think, for someone who just meets Brian, you don't know how much is there," says goalie Mike Richter, Leetch's longtime buddy and fellow New York Ranger.

"But people shouldn't confuse him being quiet with not having an opinion on something or having thought about it. He's a smart kid and a really great guy with a really, really huge heart. It's his shyness sometimes that keeps people from knowing how big it really is."

"Leetch has a remarkable knack for getting his point shot through traffic and to the net."

Richter ought to know a thing or two about the 30-year-old defenseman. He's been the best of friends with Leetch since 1985, when the two were on the U.S. Junior National Team.

"I can remember this guy who's like 140 pounds, a defenseman from Connecticut . . . He comes down, he's wiggling like Jello, going this way and that way. And I'm thinking 'What is the deal with this kid?' He sure wasn't very impressive to look at. But, man, he was smart on the ice, even back then."

Today, no one's calling Brian Leetch a kid. No one's calling the 190-pounder a lightweight.

When Leetch's name is mentioned, it's more often used in a sentence that contains words like "gifted" or "blessed" or "champion."

Consider some of the items on this guy's resume. He's twice won the Norris Trophy. He's won the Conn Smythe and the Calder Trophies. He's won the Stanley Cup and participated in the Olympics, the Canada Cup, and the World Cup of Hockey.

He's also been handed the Steve McDonald Award for being the player who goes "above and beyond the call of duty" as voted by the fans, as well as the "Good Guy" Award for cooperation with the media.

Jello, he's not.

"Leetch is a quiet leader," says the *Hockey Scouting Report* of the man who inherited the captain's insignia after Mark Messier left New York for Vancouver. "His game has matured, gained a shiny lustre like fine wood. He remains the finest player at his position and boasts the hardware—two Norris Trophies and a Conn Smythe—to prove it."

Leetch, as Richter says, is a hockey player who thinks about his game. He's regarded as a top-rate penalty killer, and a skater who has astounding lateral movement. He also has an amazing ability to rebound fully just seconds after a shift.

"Leetch has a remarkable knack for getting his point shot through traffic and to the net," says the *Report*. "He even uses his eyes to fake. He is adept at looking and/or moving in one direction, then passing the opposite way."

The 1997–98 season won't go down as Leetch's best—he finished fourth among the Rangers, with 17 goals and 33 assists for 50 points. But the previous year he finished in fine form, knocking in 20 goals and adding 58 assists for 78 points.

It was Leetch's father, Jack, who coached his son through the beginning levels of hockey: Squirt, Pee Wee, and Bantam. Brian, Jack once recalled, was the kind of player who stood apart—literally—from the rest of the pack. The tiny hockey players would swarm after the puck, as tiny hockey players typically do. Except, of course, for Brian.

"He would stay in the middle of the ice and wait for the puck to pop loose," recalled Jack. "Then he'd take off on his own."

Leetch followed his father and went to Boston College, where he led the Eagles to the Hockey East championship and was named the conference's player of the year and rookie of the year.

Leetch was selected by the Rangers in the first round of the 1986 NHL Entry Draft, but it was in 1987 that he found himself firmly under the spotlight. That was when he was appointed captain of the 1988 U.S. Olympic Team.

The shy athlete, who'd once been terrified to speak in front of his grade six class in Cheshire, Connecticut, was suddenly up on the stage.

It would be the first public appearance of many. Following the Rangers' Stanley Cup victory in 1994, Leetch appeared with Messier and Richter on the *Late Show with David Letterman*, the *Tonight Show*, the *Today Show*, and the *Howard Stern Show*. Along with Messier, he also took the Cup to Yankee Stadium, and stuck around to take a little batting practice.

Leetch also makes sure he has time to help those less fortunate than himself. He does extensive work for the Leukemia Society and the Ronald McDonald House.

He's made a difference to many—to both those who are strangers, and those who know him closely.

"I know I owe a lot of my success to Brian," says Richter. "And having been close to him for so much of our careers, I've benefited so much—not just from what he does on the ice, but also from how much he helps me off the ice."

#2 BRIAN LEETCH, New York Rangers, defense

YEAR	TEAM	LEA	REGULAR SEASON					PLAYOFF				
			GP	G	A	TP	PIM	GP	G	A	TP	PIM
1986-87	Boston Coll.	H.E.	37	9	38	47	10	.....	.....	.....	.....	
1987-88	U.S. National	.....	50	13	61	74	38	.....	.....	.....	.....	.....
	U.S. Olympic	.....	6	1	5	6	4	.....	.....	.....	.....	.....
	NY Rangers	NHL	17	2	12	14	0	.....	.....	.....	.....	.....
1988-89	NY Rangers	NHL	68	23	48	71	50	4	3	2	5	2
1989-90	NY Rangers	NHL	72	11	45	56	26	.....	.....	.....	.....	.....
1990-91	NY Rangers	NHL	80	16	72	88	42	6	1	3	4	0
1991-92	NY Rangers	NHL	80	22	80	102	26	13	4	11	15	4
1992-93	NY Rangers	NHL	36	6	30	36	26	.....	.....	.....	.....	.....
1993-94	NY Rangers	NHL	84	23	56	79	67	23	11	23	34	6
1994-95	NY Rangers	NHL	48	9	32	41	18	10	6	8	14	8
1995-96	NY Rangers	NHL	82	15	70	85	30	11	1	6	7	4
1996-97	NY Rangers	NHL	82	20	58	78	40	15	2	8	10	6
1997-98	NY Rangers	NHL	76	17	33	50	32	.....	.....	.....	.....	.....

Scott
Niedermayer

In the trash-talking world of professional sports, Scott Niedermayer of the New Jersey Devils stands out—for the soft-spoken path he's taken in becoming one of the National Hockey League's premier defenseman.

While Niedermayer has always been recognized as one of the best-skating players in the NHL, his offensive flair has been muted on a team that favored a conservative, tight-as-a-drum defensive system.

But in 1997–98, even the Devils' commitment to team defense couldn't stop Niedermayer from having his best offensive year ever. He finished second in team scoring with 14 goals and 43 assists for 57 points, ahead of veteran center Doug Gilmour. Niedermayer played several games at forward,

"I love the offensive part of the game. I like to rush and I love to score."

where his speed and instinct for seizing offensive opportunities allowed him to fit right in.

"I feel he did more offensively than he did last year," says Jacques Lemaire, who retired as Devils coach at the end of their season. "He's a more exciting player to watch offensively than last year. Some guys mature later than others and Niedermayer is very quiet."

"I love the offensive part of the game," says Scott, 24. "I like to rush and I love to score." Rushing and scoring. It's something Scott and brother Rob, the year-younger center with the Florida Panthers, have been doing all their life.

The boys were raised in Cranbrook, British Columbia. Their father, Rob, was a general practitioner at Cranbrook Regional Hospital and often served as team doctor for his boys' minor hockey teams. But it was mom, Carol, who drove the kids to hockey excellence. When they were young, she signed them up for figure skating classes to develop their skills, and she even taught a power-skating class to get them more ice time.

"The city rec department asked if I wanted to be paid," Carol remembers. "I said, 'No, just find some time for my kids to skate.'" Both boys left home at 15 to play junior hockey. Scott went to Kamloops and Rob to Medicine Hat. Each was a star, but Rob remembers it being hard to live up to the lofty standards set by his brother.

"He was a great student, he won the Memorial Cup [the junior hockey championship], he was the MVP of the Memorial Cup, he won all kinds of awards," says Rob. "People would look at me and say, 'Why can't you be as good as your brother.'"

Scott was the Canadian Hockey League and Western Hockey League scholastic player of the year in 1990–91, the same year he became the Devils first pick—third overall—in the Entry Draft. When he entered the NHL, everyone compared Niedermayer to another smooth-skating defenseman destined for the Hockey Hall of Fame—Paul Coffey. While their skating style was similar, Niedermayer was never allowed the freedom to start offensive rushes the way Coffey was in his heyday with the Edmonton Oilers.

As frustrated as Niedermayer was playing a system that stifled his natural offensive tendencies, he couldn't argue with success. And the Devils were never more successful than in 1994–95, when they won the Stanley Cup. Niedermayer played a key role in the drive to the Cup, scoring four playoff goals.

"It was such a special feeling to see Scott with that Cup in his hands," remembers Carol. "We've been very lucky, but our one wish now is to see Rob experience that same sense of accomplishment."

As kids, the Niedermayer brothers were inseparable. Nothing has changed since their arrival in the NHL. The pair share the same friends, the same interests, and many of the same off-ice pursuits. They climbed Mount Rainier in Washington and are eyeing the Himalayas. They love to fish at Kootenay Lake, where they bought three acres of land and have established summer homes.

Scott was thrilled when the Devils acquired center Doug Gilmour from Toronto. Gilmour's superior puck control and strong defensive play gave Niedermayer more confidence rushing the puck and taking offensive opportunities.

Heading into his seventh full NHL season, Niedermayer is at the top of his game. "Niedermayer has it all," says the *Hockey Scouting Report*. "Speed, balance, agility, mobility, lateral movement and strength. He has unbelievable edge for turns and eluding pursuers. Even when he makes a mistake in the offensive zone, he can get

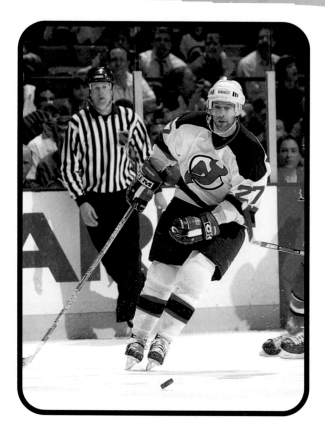

back so quickly his defense partner is seldom outnumbered."

Niedermayer's stellar play was recognized with his selection for the first time to an NHL All-Star Game. He was disappointed, however, about not being selected to the Canadian Olympic team.

With a long career still ahead of him, it's hard to imagine Niedermayer not representing his country some day at the Olympics. And if brother Rob goes too, you can bet parents Carol and Rob won't be far behind.

#27 SCOTT NIEDERMAYER, New Jersey Devils, defense

| YEAR | TEAM | LEA | REGULAR SEASON | | | | | PLAYOFFS | | | | |
			GP	G	A	TP	PIM	GP	G	A	TP	PIM
1989-90	Kamloops	WHL	64	14	55	69	64	17	2	14	16	35
1990-91	Kamloops	WHL	57	26	56	82	52	.....	.....	.....	.....	.....
1991-92	Kamloops	WHL	35	7	32	39	61	17	9	14	23	28
	New Jersey	NHL	4	0	1	1	2	.....	.....	.....	.....	.....
1992-93	New Jersey	NHL	80	11	29	40	47	5	0	3	3	2
1993-94	New Jersey	NHL	81	10	36	46	42	20	2	2	4	8
1994-95	New Jersey	NHL	48	4	15	19	18	20	4	7	11	10
1995-96	New Jersey	NHL	79	8	25	33	46	.....	.....	.....	.....	.....
1996-97	New Jersey	NHL	81	5	30	35	64	10	2	4	6	6
1997-98	New Jersey	NHL	81	14	43	57	27	6	0	2	2	4

Sandis Ozolinsh

Colorado Avalanche

Sandis Ozolinsh figures that if he wasn't in the NHL, he'd probably still be back home in Latvia, likely working in the shop his mom manages, carting around boxes.

There are times, no doubt, when he finds himself blinking twice—just to make sure this isn't all a dream. After all, when Ozolinsh was growing up in Riga, Latvia, the NHL had not penetrated those countries that were behind the so-called Soviet Iron Curtain. Whatever dreams the young athlete had did not include a professional hockey career in North America.

"How would they let a kid like me play in the NHL when they wouldn't even let Sergei Fedorov out?" says the 26-year-old Ozolinsh.

But in hockey—as in life—you can never be certain of anything.

In 1992, when Latvia underwent the transition from being a member of the Union of Soviet Socialist Republics to regaining its status as an independent Baltic state, Ozolinsh arrived in the United States. It was less than a year after he'd been picked in the second round of the NHL draft by the San Jose Sharks.

The burly defenseman—Ozolinsh is 6'3" and tips the scales at 205 pounds—first skated professionally with the Kansas City Blades of the International Hockey League. And hockey, the young man soon discovered, was a little bit different on this side of the Atlantic.

"I didn't have any idea how difficult it would be," says Ozolinsh. "There is a lot of media attention and it's difficult for young players to concentrate on their game, especially in the playoffs. I can remember in San Jose, I made a mistake and I was so afraid to talk to the media. I was trying to escape."

Ozolinsh, who spoke no English when he arrived in the U.S., discovered there were other adjustments to be made. As a younger hockey player, he'd always had a knack for scoring goals and contributing offensively. But after joining the NHL, Ozolinsh began to recognize that he had to concentrate on the mental aspects of his defensive play.

"Most of it is concentrating on my defensive zone, not to lose players," he says. "But I also have to think about when to join the rush, especially on the blueline when I have to decide to take the puck or dump it in the zone."

Ozolinsh—or "Ozo," as he's known to his friends—recorded his best season with the Sharks in 1993–94, when he scored 26 goals and added 38 assists for 64 points.

But two seasons later, the Sharks decided they were in need of a little more grit and a little more leadership and sent Ozolinsh to the Colorado Avalanche in exchange for right winger Owen Nolan.

The timing was ideal for Ozolinsh—it was the year the Avalanche would take hockey's top prize, the Stanley Cup.

The dream Ozolinsh had never dared to dream had come true.

The following year he accumulated 68 points for Colorado and was a finalist for the Norris Trophy, annually given to the league's top defenseman.

Ozolinsh, also named a starter in the 1997 NHL All-Star Game, last year led the league in goals by a defenseman, with 23. And in 1997–98, he scored 13 goals and added 38 assists for 51 points.

Now when folks look at Ozolinsh's game, they begin to realize that offense and defense aren't mutually exclusive terms.

"We get him to generate offense," says former Colorado coach Marc Crawford. "And that's what he does. He's probably one of our best chance producers. We knew exactly what we were getting when we traded for him."

It's been a long road—and an exciting journey—for the kid from Latvia, who didn't play anything but forward until he was 16.

But even now, after six seasons with the National Hockey League, and after all the records, and all the credits he's accumulated, Ozolinsh maintains that nothing comes easy to the athlete who isn't completely prepared. Success on the ice comes from hard work, both physical and mental.

Playing hockey, says Ozolinsh, is a tough way to make a living, and he's not sure he'd recommend it to sons Robert and Christopher.

"I'll let them decide what they want to do when they grow up, but I'm not going to push them into hockey. I'd hope they decide to do something other than chase a puck around."

Even so, Ozolinsh can't see himself doing anything else—and that includes carting boxes.

"I don't know of anything else I could ever do with the same enthusiasm."

#8 SANDIS OZOLINSH, Colorado Avalanche, defense

| YEAR | TEAM | LEA | REGULAR SEASON | | | | | PLAYOFFS | | | | |
			GP	G	A	TP	PIM	GP	G	A	TP	PIM
1990-91	Riga	USSR	44	0	3	3	51	.....	.....	.....	.....	.....
1991-92	Riga	CIS	30	6	0	6	42	.....	.....	.....	.....	.....
	Kansas City	IHL	34	6	9	15	20	15	2	5	7	22
1992-93	San Jose	NHL	37	7	16	23	40	.....	.....	.....	.....	.....
1993-94	San Jose	NHL	81	26	38	64	24	14	0	10	10	8
1994-95	San Jose	NHL	48	9	16	25	30	11	3	2	5	6
1995-96	San Francisco	IHL	2	1	0	1	0	.....	.....	.....	.....	.....
	San Jose	NHL	7	1	3	4	4	.....	.....	.....	.....	.....
	Colorado	NHL	66	13	37	50	50	22	5	14	19	16
1996-97	Colorado	NHL	80	23	45	68	88	17	4	13	17	24
1997-98	Colorado	NHL	66	13	38	51	65	7	0	7	7	14

Stay@Home

Defensive Defensemen

Clear The Zone

Rob Blake

Los Angeles Kings

In hockey, as in life, all things are possible. Rob Blake is proof of that. For three seasons—from 1994 to 1997—the Los Angeles defenseman was plagued with injury after injury: a torn knee ligament, an abdominal strain, a broken hand, a groin injury. It seemed he was spending more time in rehab than he was on the ice, and he began to have doubts about his future in hockey.

"There were tough stretches," recalls Blake. "You begin to wonder if you'll ever get back to the level you were at. Two years ago, when I was in rehab, I didn't think it would be possible."

Blake played just 43 percent of the time during that stretch. He was hurting—and so were the Kings. But Blake did rebound, and became a testi-

He's the most feared checker in the league.

ment to the power of personal determination and of modern medicine.

During 1997–98, Blake's first full season in four years, he won the Norris trophy as the league's top defenseman. He scored 23 goals and added 27 assists for the Kings, and was regarded as one of the main reasons why Los Angeles made the playoffs for the first time since reaching the Stanley Cup final in 1992–93. A year earlier, he helped Canada win a gold medal at the World Championship in Finland, and was named best defenseman of the tournament.

His recovery complete, the 28-year-old Blake is now being looked upon as one of the NHL's best all-round defensemen.

"He's the most feared checker in the league," notes one sports commentator.

"He's tough," says Joe Nieuwendyk of the Dallas Stars. "Tough as nails. There aren't a lot of guys in the league who put up the points he does from defense and are as good open-ice hitters."

Adds San Jose center Bernie Nicholls: "You're always aware of him physically. In our meetings before we play the Kings, our focus is on how to handle Blake. He's the best defenseman we play against, and he's having the best season of his life."

Blake, or "Blakey" as he's known to friends, is a native of Simcoe, Ontario. He played with Bowling Green University from 1987 until 1990, was drafted by the Kings in 1988, and in the spring of 1990 played his first game for Los Angeles. He was named Los Angeles' outstanding defenseman that first season, and again the next year, and the next, and the next. It was during the 1996–97 season that Blake was named captain.

Looking back, L.A. coach Larry Robinson says it's obvious that Blake has changed over the years. "When he came here, he would do things almost apologetically," recalls Robinson. "Now he takes command."

Back in the early days, fellow teammate Wayne Gretzky took one look at the youthful Blake and observed: "I don't know if he even knows how good he's going to be."

Blake, who idolized Robinson when he was a youngster, is a 6' 3", 215-pound punishing blueliner whose trademark is a brutal hip check. He can, says Robinson, "destroy somebody with a hit that turns a game around."

But Blake is also considered offensively gifted. His reflexes are rocket-quick and his slapshots are breathtaking. It seems that everyone who watches him these days is awestruck by his level of play.

"He's reacting, jumping into the play and being a physical presence," says coach Robinson. "He gives our team life with a big hit when he crunches someone."

As for Blake, he's just thrilled to be doing his bit for his team, and to be healthy and in top physical form.

"I think in the past, my injuries were just a lack of being physically at 100 percent," says Blake, who's working out more frequently in a bid to avoid future injury.

"I learned a lot from being injured, but more about being focused and how to prepare for a game. If you're going to take anything from injuries that's what I took."

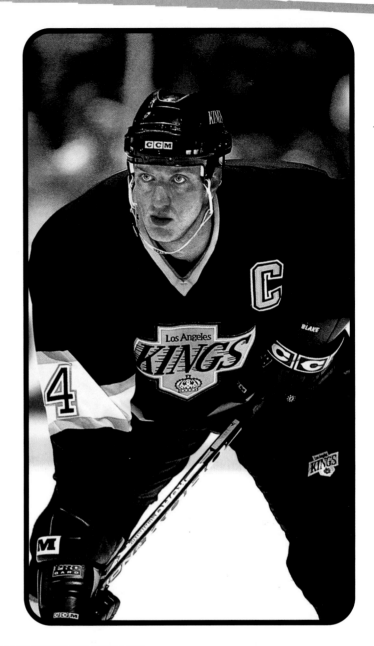

#4 ROB BLAKE, Los Angeles Kings, defense

YEAR	TEAM	LEA	REGULAR SEASON					PLAYOFFS				
			GP	G	A	TP	PIM	GP	G	A	TP	PIM
1987-88	Bowling Green	CCHA	43	5	8	13	88	.....	.....	.....	.....	.....
1988-89	Bowling Green	CCHA	46	11	21	32	140	.....	.....	.....	.....	.....
1989-90	Bowling Green	CCHA	42	23	36	59	140	.....	.....	.....	.....	.....
	Los Angeles	NHL	4	0	0	0	4	8	1	3	4	4
1990-91	Los Angeles	NHL	75	12	34	46	125	12	1	4	5	26
1991-92	Los Angeles	NHL	57	7	13	20	102	6	2	1	3	12
1992-93	Los Angeles	NHL	76	16	43	59	152	23	4	6	10	46
1993-94	Los Angeles	NHL	84	20	48	68	137	.....	.....	.....	.....	.....
1994-95	Los Angeles	NHL	24	4	7	11	38	.....	.....	.....	.....	.....
1995-96	Los Angeles	NHL	6	1	2	3	8	.....	.....	.....	.....	.....
1996-97	Los Angeles	NHL	62	8	23	31	82	.....	.....	.....	.....	.....
1997-98	Los Angeles	NHL	81	23	27	50	94	4	0	0	0	6

Nicklas Lidstrom

Detroit Red Wings

Nicklas Lidstrom admits he's no extrovert. Calm, yes. Quiet, certainly. But an attention-seeker? No way.

It just so happens, however, that an awful lot of attention has been directed lately at the Detroit defenseman. That's what tends to happen when you rack up 59 points, as Lidstrom did during the 1997–98 regular season, and place yourself second in the point total behind captain Steve Yzerman.

You kind of get noticed.

"I'm not really looking for the spotlight," says the native of Vasteras, Sweden. "I'm not avoiding it either."

Some say the spotlight focused a little more sharply on Lidstrom in 1997, during the run up to the Red Wings' first Stanley Cup victory since

1955. Late in the second game of the Western Conference final against Colorado, with the Wings leading 3-2, it was Lidstrom who knocked Eric Lacroix's shot away from the net. Moments later, Darren McCarty scored for the Wings, and Detroit was on its way to the Stanley Cup.

"I'm not really looking for the spotlight. I'm not avoiding it either."

When it was all over that year, Lidstrom brought the cup home to Sweden, along with wife Annika and sons Kevin and Adam. By the time he returned to Detroit, he discovered that things had changed considerably. Defenseman Vladimir Konstantinov had been in a limousine accident and his career was in ruins; Lidstrom was looked upon to shoulder a heavier load.

"It obviously changes things when you lose a guy like him," Lidstrom said after the accident. "But I don't mind the extra responsibility or the extra minutes. Actually, the more I play, the easier I get into the game."

Lidstrom did get increased ice time at Joe Louis and elsewhere—he sometimes played more than 30 minutes a game. And Detroit coach Scotty Bowman began to notice something remarkable about his premier defenseman: he had an ability to do a little bit of everything.

"He's producing offensively, he's out there on the power play, out there on the penalty kill, and he's matched up against the other team's best players."

Lidstrom, who was Detroit's third pick in the 1989 draft, has been with the Wings since 1991–92, the season he established a team record for most assists by a rookie defenseman, with 49. That year, he was runner-up to Pavel Bure for the Calder Trophy for outstanding rookie.

Prior to entering the NHL, he played for three years in the Swedish elite league. In early 1998, he also represented his homeland at the Olympics in Nagano, Japan.

Bob Hoffmeyer, a scout for the New Jersey Devils who is often in the Red Wings' press box, has spent a lot of time studying the way Lidstrom's game has developed.

"He's really doing the same thing," says Hoffmeyer. "But he's another year older, another year smarter, and another year more mature. He's just a very efficient player."

Ask Lidstrom's teammates about the 28-year-old's strengths, and they'll tell you they've long been aware of what he can give to the game. His positioning, they'll say, is perfect. His lateral movement is without compare. Rarely is he beaten in the one-on-one, in spite of the fact that he's not a physical defenseman.

"We wanted to keep him a sleeper," says Detroit winger Doug Brown. "But I guess the other teams know how good he is."

Defenseman Larry Murphy, who was acquired from the Toronto Maple Leafs in 1997, says Lidstrom's talent was a secret to him at one time. He didn't pick up on the Swede's ability until after he moved to Detroit.

"I didn't even know how good he was until I came here and started to watch him every night. He anticipates so well defensively and offensively. He goes through entire games without being out of position. He has the sense of being in the right spot."

In other words, he's an incredibly hard worker, a guy who takes his responsibilities seriously and concentrates on getting the job done.

The well-mannered, soft-spoken Swede does get the job done—game in and game out. And whether he likes it or not, people are taking notice. It's something Nick Lidstrom ought to get used to.

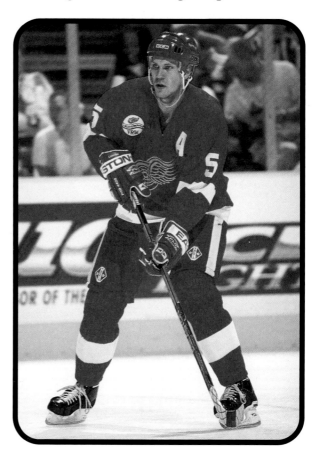

#5 NICKLAS LIDSTROM, Detroit Red Wings, defense

| YEAR | TEAM | LEA | REGULAR SEASON | | | | | PLAYOFFS | | | | |
			GP	G	A	TP	PIM	GP	G	A	TP	PIM
1987-88	Vasteras	Swe.	2	3	0	0	0	.....	.....	.....	.....	.....
1988-89	Vasteras	Swe.	19	0	2	2	4	.....	.....	.....	.....	.....
1989-90	Vasteras	Swe.	39	8	8	16	14	2	0	1	1	2
1990-91	Vasteras	Swe.	38	4	19	23	2	4	0	0	0	4
1991-92	Detroit	NHL	80	11	49	60	22	11	1	2	3	0
1992-93	Detroit	NHL	84	7	34	41	28	7	1	0	1	0
1993-94	Detroit	NHL	84	10	46	56	26	7	3	2	5	0
1994-95	Vasteras	Swe.	13	2	10	12	4	.....	.....	.....	.....	.....
	Detroit	NHL	43	10	16	26	6	18	4	12	16	8
1995-96	Detroit	NHL	81	17	50	67	20	19	5	9	14	0
1996-97	Detroit	NHL	79	15	42	57	30	20	2	6	8	2
1997-98	Detroit	NHL	80	17	42	59	18	22	6	13	19	8

Chris Pronger

Eila Pronger remembers them well, those days not so long ago when sons Sean and Chris went to battle in the basement of the family home in Dryden, Ontario. The weapons were plastic hockey sticks, the goal a cushion from the couch.

Sean always played offense, while younger brother Chris took the job of defense. They played for hours at a time.

They're still playing for hours at a time, but they've turfed the plastic sticks and returned the pillow to the chesterfield. The basement is no longer a hockey rink, but, well, part of the home on Saint Charles Street. "Now," says Eila, "there is no horsing around down there."

The boys, you see, have moved on to bigger

133

things. Bigger as in the National Hockey League.

Sean plays center for the Pittsburgh Penguins. And Chris, the kid brother who grew into a 6'5", 207-pound defenseman, is in St. Louis, where he captains the Blues and dazzles the fans, game after game.

> ## "Pronger looms on the ice, holding his position, making sure nothing untoward happens."

"He wants to dominate," says Chris's coach, Joel Quenneville. "He wants to dominate every night."

Most evenings, he does. The boy who grew up shooting a plastic puck at a pillow has traveled far. Now he appears destined to be a perennial candidate for the Norris Trophy, annually given to the league's top defenseman. Pronger was even named to the Canadian Olympic Team that traveled to

Nagano, Japan, in early 1998, and at the age of 23 was its youngest member.

Ever since Pronger was named the Canadian Hockey League's Defenseman of the Year in 1992–93, people have expected great things for him in the pros. So his Olympic assignment came as no surprise to Al MacInnis, one of Pronger's fellow Blues' defensemen.

"The way he's played the last couple of years, his development has been second to none as far as the young defensemen go," says MacInnis. "It's certainly not a surprise that he made it [to Team Canada]."

The vote of confidence must have seemed mighty sweet to Pronger, who's overcome a hurdle or two to get where he is today. When he arrived in Hartford, he had to deal with the pressure of being the 1993 No. 2 pick overall. Then he had to cope with a different set of expectations when he was traded in July 1995 to St. Louis, replacing the personable, hugely popular Brendan Shanahan. The skates were hard to fill.

But fill them he did, not Shanahan-style, but with his own personal stamp of excellence. The next season he proved to be brilliant in the playoffs.

"Chris was really under a microscope," recalls MacInnis. "Every mistake he made was scrutinized. It could have gone either way with him. It could have crushed him or it could have gone the way it has. He's developed into a strong defenseman the last two years, especially in the playoffs."

Ask Chris why things turned out the way they did and his answer is unflinchingly simple. "I didn't want to be average," he says.

In fact, he's anything but.

His strengths, say analysts, are twofold. Pronger has presence. And he has unbelievable power.

Sports Illustrated writer Michael Farber says the word "loom" applies perfectly to Pronger.

"Pronger looms on the ice, holding his position, making sure nothing untoward happens," says Farber.

The *Hockey Scouting Report* describes Pronger as a first-rate defenseman who plays more than defense.

"He blends his physical play with good offensive instincts and skills," says the *Report*. "Pronger has continued to get better every season, and in last year's playoffs was as good a defenseman as there was in the NHL."

Former Blues star Brett Hull couldn't agree more. "He's well deserving of the captaincy," says Hull. "In my 10 years here, I've never seen a guy come in and develop as he has as a player and a person. I'm so proud of him."

You can bet big brother Sean is, too. Even

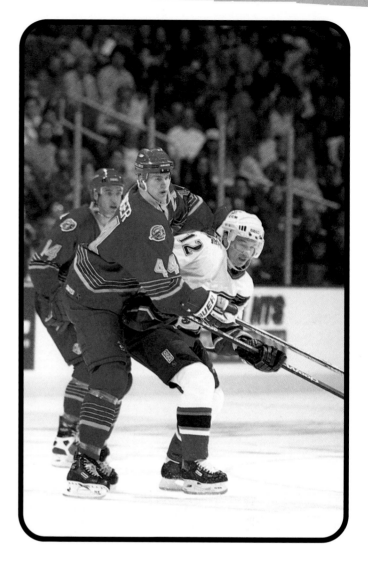

though he was Chris's basement rival at one time, and even though some of their matches turned into battles, Sean Pronger is thrilled about his brother's achievements.

"I was his biggest fan growing up," he says. "I knew he was that much better than me. Even when we were younger, he was unbelievable."

#44 CHRIS PRONGER, St. Louis Blues, defense

| YEAR | TEAM | LEA | REGULAR SEASON | | | | | PLAYOFFS | | | | |
			GP	G	A	TP	PIM	GP	G	A	TP	PIM
1991-92	Peterborough	OHL	63	17	45	62	90	10	1	8	9	28
1992-93	Peterborough	OHL	61	15	62	77	108	21	15	25	40	51
1993-94	Hartford	NHL	81	5	25	30	113	.....	.....	.....	.....	.....
1994-95	Hartford	NHL	43	5	9	14	54	.....	.....	.....	.....	.....
1995-96	St. Louis	NHL	78	7	18	25	110	13	1	5	6	16
1996-97	St. Louis	NHL	79	11	24	35	143	6	1	1	2	22
1997-98	St. Louis	NHL	81	9	27	36	180	10	1	9	10	26

Darryl Sydor

Dallas defenseman Darryl Sydor impressed Stars head coach Ken Hitchcock long before any other player on the National Hockey League team. In fact, Darryl was only 12. Hitchcock was a highly successful major junior coach in Kamloops. He'd heard about this young phenom from Edmonton, one who could skate around kids several years older.

Before Sydor was even a teenager, Hitchcock decided to include the kid on the Blazers' 50-man protected list. It was a huge gamble given the player's youth and the fact that it cost the Blazers four roster spots. It would be that number of years before Sydor could actually play in the Western Hockey League.

"I felt he had the skill to be a first-round pick in the NHL draft," Hitchcock recalls. He also remem-

bers Sydor's first camp in Kamloops. He was only 15 years old, still a year too young to play with the team but old enough for Hitchcock to get an idea of what he'd be getting the following season. Only problem was, no one told Sydor he couldn't play.

> ## "He was so distraught, he didn't understand why he hadn't made it."

"He came to camp, practiced, played some exhibition games, and then we sent him back down, like we had to," Hitchcock said. "But no one had told him he wasn't allowed to stay, so he thought he had been cut. He was so distraught, he didn't understand why he hadn't made it."

Sydor eventually got to play for Kamloops, where Hitchcock made a move with the youngster that changed his hockey career. Sydor had played forward all his life. Hitchcock, however, didn't see the finish around the net that NHL forwards needed. So he transformed Darryl into an offensive-minded defenseman. The move would pay off and Sydor, 26, would be a first-round pick (seventh overall) of the Los Angeles Kings in the 1990 Entry Draft.

In 1992–93, Sydor's first full season with Los Angeles, he got teamed up with another hot young defense prospect named Rob Blake. The two were outstanding and became a big part of the Kings' Wayne Gretzky–led march to the Stanley Cup Finals that year.

The next season, however, Blake got hurt. As is so often the case, Sydor tried to do too much in his absence. He became a high-risk, gambling defenseman. And his play soured. However, Hitchcock, now head coach of the Dallas Stars, remembered the kid who played for him in Kamloops. He believed he could be that player again and, so, engineered a trade that brought Sydor to the Stars in the latter part of the 1995–96 season.

Hitchcock's gamble paid off. Again. He got

Sydor to concentrate more on his defensive responsibilities. Once Sydor got his bearings straight, he could again pursue offensive opportunities, including a role on the vaunted Dallas power play.

In 1997–98, Sydor accumulated 46 points for the Stars on 11 goals and 35 assists. His numbers were fourth highest on the best overall team in the NHL during the regular season. It was Sydor's best season ever, putting the player on almost every coach's list of defenseman they'd love to have.

The season, however, wouldn't be without painful disappointment. Sydor lost his mother, Anne, to an aneurysm. She was only 55. There were no symptoms. Doctors said it was a congenital condition that could have struck at any time.

Darryl was devastated. The Sydor clan was extremely close, and Anne had been her son's biggest booster in his journey to the NHL. He missed three games to attend the funeral, which brought an end to his Ironman streak of 319 consecutive games.

"I can't believe it still," Sydor says now of his mother's passing. "There are things that will come to mind before a game that make me think of mom. I'll think about dad still watching at home, but now he's not watching with mom anymore."

Sydor kept the jersey from the Stars' game in Toronto, the last one his mother saw on television. He also kept the jersey from the Colorado game, which was his first after the funeral, and the puck

from the first goal he scored in Montreal after rejoining the team.

He also wears a patch on the inside of his jersey, right above his heart, that simply reads: "Mom."

"I know she's watching when I'm out there," Sydor says. "And that helps."

#5 DARRYL SYDOR, Dallas Stars, defense

YEAR	TEAM	LEA	REGULAR SEASON					PLAYOFFS				
			GP	G	A	TP	PIM	GP	G	A	TP	PIM
1988-89	Kamloops	WHL	65	12	14	26	86	15	1	4	5	19
1989-90	Kamloops	WHL	67	29	66	95	129	17	2	9	11	28
1990-91	Kamloops	WHL	66	27	78	105	88	12	3	22	25	10
1991-92	Los Angeles	NHL	18	1	5	6	22	.....	.....	.....	.....	.....
	Kamloops	WHL	29	9	39	48	43	17	3	15	18	18
1992-93	Los Angeles	NHL	80	6	23	29	63	24	3	8	11	16
1993-94	Los Angeles	NHL	84	8	27	35	94	.....	.....	.....	.....	.....
1994-95	Los Angeles	NHL	48	4	19	23	36	.....	.....	.....	.....	.....
1995-96	Los Angeles	NHL	58	1	11	12	34	.....	.....	.....	.....	.....
	Dallas	NHL	26	2	6	8	41	.....	.....	.....	.....	.....
1996-97	Dallas	NHL	82	8	40	48	51	7	0	2	2	0
1997-98	Dallas	NHL	79	11	35	46	57	17	0	5	5	14

Goalies

The Last Line of Defense

Martin Brodeur

Martin Brodeur may be the world's biggest kid.

He is, after all, just as passionate about play as he was when he was a child. Sure, he's grown a little since then: he's now 26, stands 6' 1", and weighs 205 pounds. But give Brodeur a hockey net, a stick, and a helmet, and presto: he's all boy.

"Hockey isn't only a job for Martin," says Jacques Lemaire, former coach of the New Jersey Devils. "It's his toy."

Even now, during the off-season, the Devils' prize goalie can sometimes be found on the streets outside Montreal whacking at a hockey puck.

Even now, some kid will come to the house and wonder: "Can Martin come out and play?"

"Hockey isn't only a job for Martin," says Jacques Lemaire, coach of the New Jersey Devils. "It's his toy."

As a matter of fact, he can. In 1997–98, New Jersey's netminders boasted the lowest goals-against average in the NHL, thanks largely to the efforts of Brodeur. His GAA last season was 1.89, up slightly from the 1.88 he recorded a year earlier, then the lowest GAA in the NHL since Tony Esposito's 1.77 in 1971–72. Brodeur also shut out the opposition 10 times in each of the last two years.

He's won the Calder Trophy for outstanding rookie (in 1993–94), been a runner-up for the Vezina, received the Devils' MVP award, and joined Team Canada at the Olympic Games in Nagano, Japan. Oh, yes, there was also that Stanley Cup, the one the Devils took in 1995.

And years ago, his dad could see it coming. At least, the part about Martin making it into the National Hockey League.

Hockey, after all, was always a big deal in the Brodeur household, and Denis Brodeur was one of the reasons why. Martin's dad was a celebrated goaltender in his own right—he was a bronze medal winner as starting goalie of the 1956 Canadian Olympic Team.

But by the time Martin arrived, as the youngest of five children, Denis had abandoned the net and was working as a sports photographer for both the Expos and the Canadiens. He was off the ice, but he wasn't out of the sports loop.

"My dad would talk to players like Claude Lemieux and Stephane Richer and tell them one day his son was going to play in the NHL," recalls Brodeur. "How many dads say the same thing? But gee, he was right."

Denis did know a thing or two about goaltending, but he never pushed his son too hard.

"I only went on the ice with him three or four times," says Denis. "When a kid does that well, you

don't change his style. You just add to it. The only thing I ever helped him with was the wandering aspect of being a goalie—going behind the net and coming out to clear the puck."

Even though Brodeur can't recall a time when he didn't play hockey, he does remember playing positions other than goal. At one time in his young career, he played on two teams: as goalie on one, and forward on another.

"One day, my coach said: 'You have to choose. What are you going to do, be a forward or a goalie?' It's funny now, because it was the biggest decision of my life. But I was just a little kid. So I just said, 'OK, I'll be a goalie.' "

Hockey-watchers say Brodeur's biggest strength as a goaltender may be his ability to handle pressure, no matter what's coming his way.

"What I'm impressed by, and what makes him a great goaltender, is that he stops the puck when it needs to be stopped," says New York Islanders general manager Mike Milbury. "He's cool. The pressure doesn't bother him. Night after night, he seems to be involved in 1-0, 2-1 games and the pressure never seems to be a factor."

The *Hockey Scouting Report* echoes those observations about the Montreal-born Brodeur, who started playing the game, both on the street and on the ice, when he was about four.

"Bad games and bad goals don't bother Brodeur for long," says the *Report*. "He concentrates and

doesn't lose his intensity throughout a game. Teammates love playing in front of him because of the confidence he exudes—even through the layers of padding and the mask."

Like many goalies, Brodeur has his game-day ritual: his is to get dressed from left to right. Also, he has his idols: Brodeur's has always been Patrick Roy. But unlike a lot of athletes—and for that matter, a lot of people—Brodeur is a genuinely upbeat kind of guy. He is, says sports writer Michael Farber, "350 days a year of sunshine."

"He's a first-class person," says Devils owner John McMullen.

Where goalies are concerned, he's one of a kind, says former teammate Shawn Chambers, who was Brodeur's road roommate. "Marty is one of the most normal guys I've ever been around."

#30 MARTIN BRODEUR, New Jersey Devils, goalie

YEAR	TEAM	LEA	REGULAR SEASON								PLAYOFFS						
			GP	W	L	T	MINS	GA	SO	AVG	GP	W	L	MINS	GA	SO	AVG
1989-90	St-Hyacinthe	QMJHL	42	23	13	2	2333	156	0	4.01	12	5	7	678	46	0	4.07
1990-91	St-Hyacinthe	QMJHL	52	22	24	4	2946	162	2	3.30	4	0	4	232	16	0	4.14
1991-92	New Jersey	NHL	4	2	1	0	179	10	0	3.35	1	0	1	32	3	0	5.63
	St-Hyacinthe	QMJHL	48	27	16	4	2846	161	2	3.39	5	2	3	317	14	0	2.65
1992-93	Utica	AHL	32	14	13	5	1952	131	0	4.03	4	1	3	258	18	0	4.19
1993-94	New Jersey	NHL	47	27	11	8	2625	105	3	2.40	17	8	9	1171	38	1	1.95
1994-95	New Jersey	NHL	40	19	11	3	2184	89	3	2.45	20	16	4	1222	34	3	1.67
1995-96	New Jersey	NHL	77	34	30	12	4433	173	6	2.34	....	....		....	....	....	....
1996-97	New Jersey	NHL	67	37	14	13	3838	120	10	1.88	10	5	5	659	19	2	1.73
1997-98	New Jersey	NHL	70	43	17	8	4128	130	10	1.89	6	2	4	366	12	0	1.97

Dominik Hasek

Buffalo Sabres

The whole of the Czech Republic was roaring with joy that Sunday morning in early 1998. They were celebrating something that was happening half a world away, in Nagano, Japan.

The Czechs had just defeated the Russians 1-0 to win Olympic gold. And more than anyone, it was goaltender Dominik Hasek who'd been responsible for the victory.

"Hasek to the castle!" screamed the thousands upon thousands of Czechs who gathered in Prague's Old Town Square to greet Hasek and his teammates after they flew in from Nagano. They were suggesting that Hasek ought to take on the job of president.

But no, said Hasek politely when President Vaclav Havel telephoned him after the game to say he was looking forward to trading places. The celebrated Buffalo Sabres goalie said he wasn't planning on giving up his job.

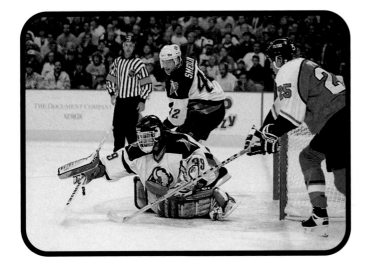

Within professional hockey, Hasek was already a hot item. After all, he'd already won the Hart Trophy the previous June, becoming the first goalie in 35 years to win the award for the NHL's most valuable player. He'd already won three Vezinas and the Lester B. Pearson Award as the MVP as chosen by the players.

"I feel like I'm traveling with the Beatles or Elvis," said Gilbert. "He's like a rock star."

But with Olympic gold came instant worldwide acclaim. There were invitations to do interviews with Fox News, with CNN, with MTV. Hasek became a celebrity in the days and weeks after Nagano, and no one knew that better than Sabres director of communications Mike Gilbert.

"I feel like I'm traveling with the Beatles or Elvis," said Gilbert. "He's like a rock star."

Everyone, it seems, was echoing the words of Richard Smehlik, a teammate of Hasek's, both on the Sabres and on Team Czech. "He is," said Smehlik, "the best goalie in the world. Ever."

Absolutely, said Jaromir Jagr of the Pittsburgh Penguins, also a member of the Czech gold-medal team. "He's the best. We've got the best goalie in the world."

Hasek says the three days in Nagano, during which the Czechs triumphed over the U.S., Canada, and finally the Russians, will go down as the best days of his life. But The Dominator is clearly uncomfortable when asked who ranks as the No. 1 goaltender.

"I hate those questions," says the 33-year-old native of Pardubice, an industrial town of 100,000 in the northeast of the Czech Republic. "I just want to prove every day that I am a good goalie. I never feel like I am the best. Maybe I am. I don't know. I let other people think about that."

People have been thinking about that—about Hasek's superstar ability—both before and after the Olympics. It's hard not to notice a guy who recorded 13 regular season shutouts in 1997–98, 6 of them in a single month, and finished up with a goals-against average of 2.09.

Hasek is recognized as a fierce competitor who possesses an almost impenetrable level of concentration when he's is in the net.

"I bet he doesn't hear a sound when he's playing," says John Muckler, former general manager of the Sabres, now coach of the Rangers. "That's how hard he concentrates."

Hasek, who stands 5' 11" and weighs just 168 pounds, has mastered the positioning, and the anticipation, and possesses an almost eerie level of flexibility.

"He sits on the floor, spreads his legs, bends at the waist—and touches his stomach to the floor," says Buffalo center Mike Peca. "Like a contortionist."

Hasek, once described by a Czech writer as the goaltending equivalent of Mozart, says as far back as he can remember, he always wanted to be in the net. And one day, when he was just six, his father took him to a hockey tryout.

"I didn't even have real skates," he says. "I had those blades that you screwed onto the soles of your shoes, but I was tall and the nine-year-olds didn't have a goalie, so they put me in with them." From then on, Hasek always played with the older boys.

His flexibility immediately attracted attention: he

could do a kneeling split, and was double-jointed.

Hasek had no goalie coach, so he became his own teacher. "When I was 10 or 11, I'd go and watch the practices of the junior team. And I'd just pay attention to what the goalie was doing and think about it. I'd look for things that worked and for things that didn't. And then I'd try them out in my practices."

By the time Hasek was 16, he made Pardubice Tesla, the town's pro team. For five of the eight years he played with them, he was named Czech goalie of the year.

In 1990, Hasek made the move to the NHL, joining the Chicago Blackhawks. Two years later, he became a Buffalo Sabre. Hasek played primarily behind Grant Fuhr in his first season with Buffalo, but the next year he stopped pucks from everywhere and ended up with a 1.95 goals-against average.

Ever since, Hasek has been the mainstay of the Sabres' netminding.

And ever since, the hockey world has been coming around to thinking that this is a goaltender with exceptional ability: a player who combines outstanding athleticism with intellectual discipline.

"He doesn't have a weakness and you don't know what he's going to do," says Wayne Gretzky. "There's no book on him. You can usually look at a goalie and say you can go here or there. You can't say that with Dominik."

#39 DOMINIK HASEK, Buffalo Sabres, goalie

YEAR	TEAM	LEA	REGULAR SEASON								PLAYOFFS						
			GP	W	L	T	MINS	GA	SO	AVG	GP	W	L	MINS	GA	SO	AVG
1981-82	Pardubice	Czech	12	....	....	....	661	34	....	3.09	....	....	....	....	....	....	....
1982-83	Pardubice	Czech	42	....	....	....	2358	105	....	2.67	....	....	....	....	....	....	....
1983-84	Pardubice	Czech	40	....	....	....	2304	108	....	2.81	....	....	....	....	....	....	....
1984-85	Pardubice	Czech	42	....	....	....	2419	131	....	3.25	....	....	....	....	....	....	....
1985-86	Pardubice	Czech	45	....	....	....	2689	138	....	3.08	....	....	....	....	....	....	....
1986-87	Pardubice	Czech	43	....	....	....	2515	103	....	2.46	....	....	....	....	....	....	....
1987-88	Pardubice	Czech	31	....	....	....	1862	93	....	3.00	....	....	....	....	....	....	....
1988-89	Pardubice	Czech	42	....	....	....	2507	114	....	2.73	....	....	....	....	....	....	....
1989-90	Dukla Jihlava	Czech	40	....	....	....	2251	80	....	2.13	....	....	....	....	....	....	....
1990-91	Chicago	NHL	5	3	0	1	195	8	0	2.46	3	0	0	69	3	0	2.61
	Indianapolis	IHL	33	20	11	1	1903	80	5	2.52	1	1	0	60	3	0	3.00
1991-92	Chicago	NHL	20	10	4	1	1014	44	1	2.60	3	0	2	158	8	0	3.04
	Indianapolis	IHL	20	7	10	3	1162	69	1	3.56	....	....	....	....	....	....	....
1992-93	Buffalo	NHL	28	11	10	4	1429	75	0	3.15	1	1	0	45	1	0	1.33
1993-94	Buffalo	NHL	58	30	20	6	3358	109	7	1.95	7	3	4	484	13	2	1.61
1994-95	Pardubice	Czech	2	....	....	....	124	6	0	2.90	....	....	....	....	....	....	....
	Buffalo	NHL	41	19	14	7	2416	85	5	2.11	5	1	4	309	18	0	3.50
1995-96	Buffalo	NHL	59	22	30	6	3417	161	2	2.83	....	....	....	....	....	....	....
1996-97	Buffalo	NHL	67	37	20	10	4037	153	5	2.27	3	1	1	153	5	0	1.96
1997-98	Buffalo	NHL	72	33	23	13	4220	147	13	2.09	15	10	5	948	32	1	2.03

Nikolai Khabibulin

Phoenix Coyotes

Teammates will always remember the night Phoenix Coyotes goaltender Nikolai Khabibulin truly arrived in the National Hockey League. It was April 26, 1996, and the Coyotes were then the Winnipeg Jets. Winnipeg was facing elimination from the playoffs, down three games to one to the Detroit Red Wings. And the boys from Motown wanted to finish things off. They gave it their best shot.

The Wings threw everything at Khabibulin but some of the famed octopus that still occasionally showers the Detroit ice after a goal. When the game was over, Detroit had peppered the Jets goal with 52 shots. Khabibulin would let only one past him, helping his team stave off elimination for one more game. The goalie from Sverdlovsk, Russia, was brilliant.

"I've played nine years in the league and I've seen a lot of games," said Kris King, a member of the Jets at the time. "But I've never seen a guy win a game like that. I've never seen a goalie play like that." Phoenix captain Keith Tkachuk, a teammate of Khabibulin at the time, said his play was sensational, unbelievable, you name it. "Think of the best word ever," said Tkachuk. "The way he played was just unreal." Khabibulin, 25, would go on to record many brilliant performances after that special night in Detroit, securing his position as the Coyotes' No. 1 backstopper, now and for the future.

He's been dubbed "The Bulin Wall" by the media.

Every player in the NHL has a unique story about his journey to the best hockey league in the world. And Khabibulin certainly has his. He was drafted by the Jets in the eighth round (204th overall) of the 1992 Entry Draft. But listen to how it happened. When it was the Jets turn to pick, direc-

tor of scouting Bill Lesuk asked the team's communications assistant, Igor Kuperman, to take a look at the Russians remaining. Kuperman's eyes lit up when he saw Khabibulin's name still available. So the Jets grabbed him.

The 6' 1", 176 pounder spent the next two seasons playing in Russia before making it to North America. In 1994, he made a favorable impression at the Jets training camp as he tried to adjust to a different world and a different game.

"My biggest adjustment was learning the language, so I took courses that were offered by the team," said Khabibulin. "On the ice, I had to learn to play the North American style. I had to adjust to the number of games we played and be ready to play again even if I had played poorly the night before. The ice is smaller, making the game more intense. And players are so motivated to win the Stanley Cup."

In 1995–96, his first full season in the NHL, Khabibulin played in 53 games. He won 26 with a goals-against average of 3.13. For his performance, he earned the Jets' Most Valuable Player award, amazing considering he had to beat out Tkachuk who scored 50 goals and had 98 points.

He's adjusted nicely to both the league and a new country and culture. Teammates call him Nik or Habby. He's been dubbed "The Bulin Wall" by the media. His last name is pronounced Habby-boo-lin, which some hockey broadcasters around the league still occasionally trip over.

"It's not that hard to say," Khabibulin once said about his name. "Anyway, I don't care. People will learn my name if I play well."

Sverdlovsk is a city of about 1.5 million people, located near the Ural Mountains, about a two-hour flight from Moscow. Khabibulin grew up in a middle-class Russian family with a sports-oriented atmosphere. His father was a high jumper, his mother a runner. From an early age, Nikolai played soccer, tennis, handball, and hockey. He didn't start skating on a rink until he was 10. As a young hockey player, Khabibulin played defense. But when he was 14 he read a book by Russian goaltending great, Vladislav Tretiak. It inspired him to make the move to goal.

Russian goaltenders were taught to stay back in their nets, in stark contrast to the technique being drilled into North American net-minders, which was to go out and challenge shooters. Luckily for Khabibulin, he didn't always listen to his coaches.

"I fooled them. I practiced coming out of the net when they weren't watching," Khabibulin remembers. "It made me better prepared to play in the NHL. You stop the puck. It's the same in any language."

He admires NHL goaltenders Patrick Roy and Ed Belfour; however, his style mostly compares to Toronto Maple Leafs backstopper Curtis Joseph.

"His style is half-standup and half-butterfly," says former Phoenix GM John Paddock. "But mostly, he is really agile." Former Coyotes coach Don Hay says Khabibulin is terrific at challenging the shooter.

"And he's got the reflexes to respond to anything going across the ice. He's used to that from Europe but he has adjusted to the North American style."

Since joining the league, Khabibulin's goals-against average has dropped each season. From 3.41 during a partial rookie season to 3.13, to 2.83 in 1996–97 and 2.74 in 70 games this past season.

His consistently stellar play was recognized this past season as Khabibulin appeared in his first NHL All-Star Game. Coyotes GM Bobby Smith

said the honor finally put the Phoenix goalie among hockey's best.

"The exposure comes from just being there and being one of the elite," said Smith. "His presence in the game is a heck of a statement on the type of goalie we have."

Nikolai Khabibulin is indeed one of the best.

#35 NIKOLAI KHABIBULIN, Phoenix Coyotes, goalie

YEAR	TEAM	LEA	GP	W	L	T	MINS	GA	SO	AVG	GP	W	L	MINS	GA	SO	AVG
							REGULAR SEASON					PLAYOFFS					
1988-89	Sverdlovsk	USSR	1	....	....	....	3	0	0	0.00	....	....	....	....	....	....	....
1989-90	Sverdlovsk, Jrs.	USSR						UNAVAILABLE										
1990-91	Sputnik	USSR 3						UNAVAILABLE										
1991-92	CSKA	CIS	2	....	....	....	34	2	....	3.52	....	....	....	....	....	....	....
1992-93	CSKA	CIS	13	....	....	....	491	27	....	2.65	....	....	....	....	....	....	....
1993-94	CSKA	CIS	46	....	....	....	2625	116	....	2.65	3	....	....	193	11	....	3.42
	Russian Pens	IHL	12	2	7	2	639	47	0	4.41	....	....	....	....	....	....	....
1994-95	Springfield	AHL	23	9	9	3	1240	80	0	3.87	....	....	....	....	....	....	....
	Winnipeg	NHL	26	8	9	4	1339	76	0	3.41	....	....	....	....	....	....	....
1995-96	Winnipeg	NHL	53	26	20	3	2914	152	2	3.13	6	2	4	359	19	0	3.18
1996-97	Phoenix	NHL	72	30	33	6	4091	193	7	2.83	7	3	4	426	15	1	2.11
1997-98	Phoenix	NHL	70	30	28	10	4026	184	4	2.74	4	2	1	185	13	0	4.22

Patrick Roy

Colorado Avalanche

Colorado Avalanche general manager Pierre Lacroix had never seen it before. Sure, he'd observed determination in an athlete. He'd seen commitment. But when he got to know Patrick Roy he noticed something more intense, more striking than he'd ever seen.

"In my 20 years in this game, I've seen some great players and some great people," says Lacroix. "But I have never seen anyone with Patrick Roy's drive to win. I have never seen anyone who hated to lose as much as Patrick Roy.

"That's something you can't invent or create. That's something that's inside you, and it's always been inside Patrick."

Lacroix isn't into making hasty observations; he's known Roy since Roy was 16. And more than anyone, it was Lacroix who celebrated on December 6,

1995, when Roy was acquired from the Montreal Canadiens by the Avalanche, along with Mike Keane, in exchange for Jocelyn Thibault, Martin Rucinsky, and Andrei Kovalenko. Lacroix knew Colorado was not simply picking up a goaltender. It was also acquiring a leader, a champion, a hero.

"I have never seen anyone who hated to lose as much as Patrick Roy."

He had, after all, worked the net during two rides by Montreal to the Stanley Cup championship. He'd won two Conn Smythe Trophies and three Vezinas. So driven is Roy that in 1994 he was determined to work his magic in the first round of the playoffs—in spite of an appendicitis attack. He missed the third game of the series against Boston, but convinced doctors to let him return for the fourth game on antibiotics. Roy made the game, and stopped 39 shots to lead the Canadiens to a 5-2 victory.

To Montrealers, the native of Quebec City was not just a king. He was also "Saint Patrick."

But all good things, as the saying goes, must come to an end—and Roy's relationship with the Canadiens was no exception.

The party ended in a much-publicized dispute on December 2, 1995, after Montreal lost in an 11-1 blowout against Detroit. Embarrassed that he hadn't been yanked from the net as the goals mounted, he skated to the bench and pointed at team president Ronald Corey.

"That was the last game I will ever play for the Montreal Canadiens," he said. And it was. Four days later he was shipped to Colorado.

The leave-taking was tough—it was a difficult way to bid adieu to Montreal. But within a few months, Roy noticed that things began to turn around.

"I'm the happiest guy in the world," Roy said months after the move. "I've got to be honest. It's turned out to be the nicest thing that could happen to me."

No wonder. The first year Roy was with the Avalanche he added another Stanley Cup ring to his collection. In 1996–97, he led the NHL in wins with 38, was a finalist for yet another Vezina, and was voted Denver's top athlete in a reader's poll. And in the 1997–98 season, the year Roy represented Canada at the Winter Olympics in Nagano,

Japan, he recorded 31 wins, including four shutouts, and had a goals-against average of 2.39.

It has also helped that the off-ice transition has gone well. Roy's wife, Michele, and three children have had to work at improving their English, but they've been impressed with the way their new community has welcomed them.

"I thought, well, we'll move back to Montreal when my career is done, but now I'm not so sure," says Roy, who'll be 33 in October. "We might just want to stay. It's such a nice, pretty state, and the people are nice."

Roy is the kind of athlete who loves to be among his fans, especially the kids. He still recalls that day when he was a child and he met his own hockey hero, Daniel Bouchard. The former Quebec Nordiques goalie gave Roy his stick, and Roy slept with it for nights after that.

"I try to look at every kid now who approaches me as that same kid that I was," says Roy, a big contributor to the Ronald McDonald house.

If Roy is known for his fan accessibility, he's also known for his quirky superstitions. He won't skate on the red or blue lines, he writes his kids' names on his stick before each game, and he stores the pucks from his current season shutouts in his locker until the end of the season.

It remains to be seen whether the superstitions work. But there's no question that something does.

Patrick Roy, hockey hero, is the man his team relies upon. "When your goalie is Patrick Roy," says Avalanche defenseman Sylvain Lefebvre, "when you look back there and see him in the net, it's an incredible feeling. You just know everything's going to be all right."

#33 PATRICK ROY, Colorado Avalanche, goalie

YEAR	TEAM	LEA	REGULAR SEASON								PLAYOFFS						
			GP	W	L	T	MINS	GA	SO	AVG	GP	W	L	MINS	GA	SO	AVG
1982-83	Granby	QMJHL	54	13	35	1	2808	293	0	6.26	....	....	....	....	....	....	....
1983-84	Granby	QMJHL	61	29	29	1	3585	265	0	4.44	4	0	4	244	22	0	5.41
1984-85	Montreal	NHL	1	1	0	0	20	0	0	0.00	....	....	....	....	....	....	....
	Granby	QMJHL	44	16	25	1	2463	228	0	5.55	....	....	....	....	....	....	....
	Sherbrooke	AHL	1	1	0	0	60	4	0	4.00	13	10	3	769	37	0	2.89
1985-86	Montreal	NHL	47	23	18	3	2651	148	1	3.35	20	15	5	1218	39	1	1.92
1986-87	Montreal	NHL	46	22	16	6	2686	131	1	2.93	6	4	2	330	22	0	4.00
1987-88	Montreal	NHL	45	23	12	9	2586	125	3	2.90	8	3	4	430	24	0	3.35
1988-89	Montreal	NHL	48	33	5	6	2744	113	4	2.47	19	13	6	1206	42	2	2.09
1990-91	Montreal	NHL	48	25	15	6	2835	128	1	2.71	13	7	5	785	40	0	3.06
1991-92	Montreal	NHL	67	36	22	8	3935	155	5	2.36	11	4	7	686	30	1	2.62
1992-93	Montreal	NHL	62	31	25	5	3595	192	2	3.20	20	16	4	1293	46	0	2.13
1993-94	Montreal	NHL	68	35	17	11	3867	161	7	2.50	6	3	3	375	16	0	2.56
1994-95	Montreal	NHL	43	17	20	6	2566	127	1	2.97	....	....	....	....	....	....	....
1995-96	Montreal	NHL	22	12	9	1	1260	62	1	2.95	....	....	....	....	....	....	....
	Colorado	NHL	39	22	15	1	2305	103	1	2.68	22	16	6	1454	51	3	2.10
1996-97	Colorado	NHL	62	38	15	7	3698	143	7	2.32	17	10	7	1034	38	3	2.21
1997-98	Colorado	NHL	65	31	19	13	3835	153	4	2.39	7	3	4	403	18	0	2.51

10 to Watch

JASON ALLISON
F Boston Bruins

The kind of center every team wants. Big, skilled, and tough. Will be in the league a long time.

BRYAN BERARD
D New York Islanders

Former rookie-of-the-year looks to be surefire Norris Trophy candidate in years to come.

ANSON CARTER
F Boston Bruins

Has power, speed, and great hands. His future in the league has never looked brighter.

JERE LEHTINEN
F Dallas Stars

A player every coach wants on his team. One of the league's premier defensive forwards who combines speed with tenacity.

MIKE JOHNSON
F Toronto Maple Leafs
One of the top rookies in 1997–98. Looks to become one of the players the Leafs will build around.

JAMIE LANGENBRUNNER
F Dallas Stars
Combines toughness with finesse. Will be a force on the Stars for years to come.

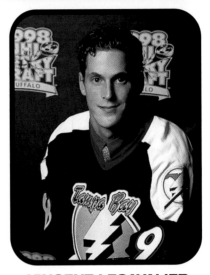

VINCENT LECAVALIER
F Tampa Bay Lightning
The 6'4" No. 1 choice overall in the 1998 draft is predicted to be a franchise player in the mold of Mario Lemieux.

MIKE GRIER
F Edmonton Oilers
Quickly becoming one of the top power forwards in the league.

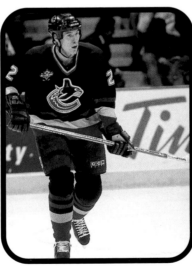

MATTIAS OHLUND
D Vancouver Canucks
Calder Trophy finalist, the smooth-skating Swede has the total package to become one of the league's premier blueliners.

SERGEI SAMSONOV
F Boston Bruins
Last season's rookie of the year proved he's for real. He makes moves league veterans have never seen.

Photo Credits

All photographs were provided by Allsport Photography (USA)

Brian Bahr, 32, 40, 41, 42, 43, 86, 106, 107, 108, 154, 156, 157
Steve Babineau, 89, 115, 158
Al Bello, 16, 78, 79, 81, 113, 114, 133, 142, 149, 155
Simon Bruty, 112, 132
M. Campanelli/B. Bennett Studios, 159
Graham Chadwick, 70
Glenn Cratty, 33, 63, 97, 127, 137
Stephen Dunn, 12, 14, 36, 62, 102, 111, 129, 138, 159
Otto Greule Jr., 24, 27
Elsa Hasch, 9, 11, 25, 26, 35, 44, 45, 47, 72, 84, 99, 100, 103, 119, 124, 125, 128, 130, 131, 136, 150, 151, 158
Harry How, 39
Jed Jacobsohn, 121, 126
Craig Jones, 30, 95
Robert Laberge, 8, 18, 21, 48, 51, 55, 60, 85, 88, 93, 94, 116, 143, 146, 153, 158
Joe Mahoney 10, 109
Ted Mathias, 66
Craig Melvin, 23, 28, 87
Doug Pensinger, 54, 56, 57, 134, 135, 159
Nevin Reid, 34, 73, 77, 118, 120, 152
Ezra O. Shaw, 17, 117, 158
Jamie Squire, 76
Rick Stewart, 19, 20, 29, 38, 46, 49, 50, 64, 65, 67, 68, 75, 90, 91, 92, 96, 98, 101, 110, 144, 147, 148
Damian Strohmeyer, 145
Ian Tomlinson, 13, 15, 31, 37, 61, 139, 159
Jeff Vinnick, 22, 58, 74, 80
Todd Warshaw, 59, 69, 71,

Cover photo credit: Rick Stewart/ Al Bello

Acknowledgements

Virtually all the quotes contained in this book first appeared in newspapers, magazines, and in-house publications of NHL teams throughout the United States and Canada. The authors would like to thank:

The Arizona Republic
Avalanche Game Magazine
The Buffalo News
The Calgary Herald
The Calgary Sun
The Canadian Press
Chicago Sun-Times
Cigar Aficionado
Dallas Morning News
Dallas Stars Game Magazine
Details
The Detroit Free Press
The Detroit News
The Denver Post
The Edmonton Journal
The Edmonton Sun
Greensboro News and Record
The Hartford Courant
Hockey Digest
The Hockey News
The Hockey Scouting Report
Hockey Superstars
Inside Hockeytown
The L.A. Times
Long Beach Press Telegram
Men's Journal
Mesa Tribune
The Montreal Gazette
Newark Star-Ledger
The News and Observer
The New York Daily News
The New York Post
The New York Times
NHL Powerplay
The Orange County Register

The Ottawa Citizen
The Ottawa Sun
The Pittsburgh Post-Gazette
The Pittsburgh Tribune Review
The Province
The Rocky Mountain News
The Salt Lake Tribune
San Francisco Chronicle
San Jose Mercury News
San Jose Sharks Magazine
The Sporting News
Sports Illustrated
The St. Louis Post-Dispatch
The Tampa Tribune
The Toronto Star
The Toronto Sun
The Vancouver Sun
Washington Times
The Washington Post
Winnipeg Free Press
USA Today

The authors wish to add a special thanks to staff members of the Pacific Press Library for their invaluable research assistance.